# ON NOT LEAVING IT TO THE SNAKE

by Harvey G. Cox

THE SECULAR CITY
GOD'S REVOLUTION AND MAN'S RESPONSIBILITY

# ON
# NOT LEAVING IT
# TO THE SNAKE

by HARVEY G. COX

SCM PRESS LTD

LONDON

Acknowledgment is made to the following for permission to reprint from previously published material:
William Robert Miller for "The Death of God and the Future of Theology," copyright © 1967 by William Robert Miller, from *The New Christianity*, edited by William Robert Miller (New York: Delacorte Press, 1967); The Christian Century Foundation for "The Place and Purpose of Theology" from the January 5, 1966, issue of *The Christian Century*, copyright 1966 by The Christian Century Foundation, and reprinted in *Frontline Theology*, edited by Dean Peerman, © M. E. Bratcher 1967 (Richmond, Va.: John Knox Press), "The Gospel and the Postliterate Man" from the November 25, 1964, issue of *The Christian Century*, copyright 1964 by The Christian Century Foundation, and "Let's End the Communist-Christian Vendetta" from the November 9, 1966, issue of *The Christian Century*, copyright 1966 by The Christian Century Foundation; Christianity and Crisis, Inc., for "The Church in East Germany" from the July 22, 1963, issue of *Christianity and Crisis*, and "New Phase in the Marxist-Christian Encounter" from the November 1, 1965, issue of *Christianity and Crisis*, copyright 1965 by Christianity and Crisis, Inc.; Commonweal Publishing Co., Inc., for "Kafka, East and West" from the September 4, 1964, issue of *Commonweal*, copyright 1964 by the Commonweal Publishing Co., Inc.; The Andover Newton Theological School for "The Changing Scene in Evangelism" from the June 1960 issue of the *Andover Newton Quarterly*; The Ministers and Missionaries Benefit Board of the American Baptist Convention for "The Coming World City" originally entitled "Mission in a World of Cities"; The Confraternity of Christian Doctrine for "The Restoration of a Sense of Place" from the Fall 1965 issue of *The Living Light*, copyright 1965 by The Confraternity of Christian Doctrine; The Journal of American Academy of Arts and Sciences for "The New Breed in American Churches: Sources of Social Activism in American Religion" from the Winter 1967 issue of *Daedalus*, Vol. 96, No. 1; The United Church of Canada for "Where Is the Church Going and How Is It Going to Get There" from *The Observer*, 1967 Centennial Reference Issue; The National Conference of Christians and Jews, Inc., for "The Statute of Limitations on Nazi Crimes" originally published and distributed in *Background Reports*, June 1965.

# Contents

# PART THREE

## RECOGNIZING THE NEW ERA—THE CHURCH AND THE FUTURE

# ADDENDUM

## THE STATUTE OF LIMITATIONS ON NAZI CRIMES

# Introduction:
# Faith and Decision

ALTHOUGH HE SELDOM THINKS ABOUT IT, MAN KNOWS HIMSELF AS that animal who must make decisions. He clicks off little choices every day: which tie to wear, which chore to tackle first at the office, which TV channel to flip to in the evening. Once in a while he confronts larger choices: whether to change jobs, how to cope with marital strife, what he can do about a problem child. Occasionally his fantasies tease him with choices he will never have to make: what he would do if he were President of the United States, if he were the Pope, if he were starting all over again at sixteen. Human life is made of decisions.

True, the average person turns many of his decisions over to habit, instinct, or peer group pressure. No Wall Street financier really considers wearing a six inch wide cerise tie to work. Few South Boston Irish voters think seriously about voting for a Cabot against a Houlihan. We are glad to let the clothes salesman tell us what is and what isn't being worn this season.

But we are not entirely creatures of habit and group suggestion. And there's the rub. Somewhere deep down we know that in the final anaysis we *do* decide things and that even our decisions to let someone else decide are really *our* decisions, however pusillanimous. We know that as human beings we *are* creatures of decision and that in some way we are responsible for the choices we make.

But how does faith relate to this characteristically human process of decision-making? For people whose academic specialty is the study of religion and ethics, this question is an enormously complex one. It could not be answered short of a thick theological tome. But for most ordinary people the answer is all too simple: our religion tells us what is right and what is wrong. Of course we do have to "apply" its general precepts to sticky specific situations, which is often a baffling business. But the "right answer" is there if we try hard enough. It is "there" in the Bible, Ten Commandments, Canon Law, Encyclicals, Golden Rule, or somewhere. But of course we don't always *do* the right thing, this conventional religion concedes, and Christianity provides us with a way out. The doctrine of original sin gives us some comfort by suggesting that we had two strikes against us before we began. Confessing and being forgiven helps get us back on the straight and narrow path. For many people the relationship between faith and decision never gets much beyond this.

At a more sophisticated level some religious people misuse the notion of original sin almost as a way to avoid taking responsibility for the decisions they must make. They insist that the most dangerous of all human sins is pride. Man's perversity is that he tries to be more than man. He refuses to accept his dependent status, resents "the way things are," and chafes under the limitations imposed on him by reality. The good Christian therefore turns out to be the one who doesn't expect too much of himself, adjusts to the seemingly given conditions around him, and is content with his lot. He is the man who, as it were, knows his place in the scheme of things and reconciles himself to it. Our faith helps us accept ourselves as the weak, ineffective, and basically powerless creatures we are.

The essays collected in this book all express in one way or another my conviction that this popular notion of the place of faith in human decision-making is distorted and misleading. Because it is so widespread, however, it causes real mischief and needs to be challenged as cogently as possble. I do *not* believe biblical faith relates to decision by providing a sure-fire method of discriminating right from wrong. I do *not* believe that Christianity should be expected to equip us with a set of generalized ethical rules which we seek to apply in various situations. I think our overemphasis on the guilt-and-forgiveness aspect of Christianity has nearly obscured the fact that the gospel is first of all a call to leave the past behind and open ourselves to the promise of the future. I think it is wrong and dangerous for the church to continue to pound away at pride as the tragic human flaw and to make a virtue of dependency.

What I want to say about faith and decision is something quite different. Man is summoned to make his own decisions. So to shove them off on someone else, even on God or the church, is a betrayal of his manhood. True, the Bible and the Christian tradition are alive with ethical insights and moral wisdom. They are misused, however, if they are made to function as eternally applicable canons that excuse us from the frightful responsibility of renewing and reconstructing our moral tradition in the light of unprecedented issues our forebears never had to confront: the bomb, the computer, the pill. I believe a careful examination of the biblical sources will indicate that man's most debilitating proclivity is *not* his pride. It is *not* his attempt to be more than man. Rather it is his sloth, his unwillingness to be everything man was intended to be. His moral discoloration stems only in part from his unwillingness to be sorry for the wrong he has done in the past. It stems even more from his unwillingness to take responsibility for what he will do in the future.

To clarify the relation between faith and decision we need

today, among other things, a doctrine of sin that will not encourage deference and dependency. We need a truly contemporary version of what virtue and sainthood mean. We need a vision of man that celebrates his unique role in the cosmos and his unavoidable responsibility for the future. We can start this process with a critical reexamination of the conventional conceptions of man as sinner and man as saint.

Man-as-sinner has usually been pictured by religious writers as man-the-insurrectionary, the proud heaven-storming rebel who has not learned to be content with his lot. Refined and escalated in literature, this image blossoms in the heroic Satans and Lucifers of Goethe and Milton. No wonder we find sin so interesting and sinners more attractive than saints. No wonder we secretly admire Lucifer while our orthodox doctrine condemns him to the lake of fire. This misleading view of sin as pride and rebelliousness has given the very word sin an intriguing lustre: a naked Eve with moist bedroom eyes guiltily tasting the forbidden apple; a slithery, clearly phallic, serpent; man defying the petty conventions imposed on him by small-minded people. In these terms why shouldn't we be in favor of sin?

The only trouble in this mishmash of sex and self-affirmation images has almost nothing to do with the biblical idea of sin. It is basically a Greek, or more precisely, promethean, notion larded with remnants of medieval folk piety, Victorian antisexuality, and the bourgeois obsession with orderliness. Since far too much of our picture of the saint is negatively defined by our picture of the sinner, it is no surprise that saints seem so pale and tedious in comparison.

Ironically our distortion of the idea of sin has produced almost the opposite of its intention: nobody wants to be a saint nowadays, though everyone would like to be a "sinner," if he had the gumption or the opportunity.

But the situation is not hopeless. While popular religion and even many theologians have been perpetrating this distorted doctrine of sin, our men of letters have already pushed on to a new and more authentic vision. They have begun to chisel out new models of the saint and the sinner, models that turn out to be much more in keeping with the biblical grain. In the writings of T. S. Eliot, who was a lonely pioneer in this massive redefinition, there was never anything promethean about sin. Eliot looked out on a gray world populated not by brazen privateers but by hollow men and carbuncular clerks. His insight into the real sickness of our age, as it limps toward a whimper instead of a bang, is still accurate. Franz Kafka chills even the most insulated marrow with his parable of the humdrum office clerk whose first thought, when he discovers he has been transformed into a loathsome caterpillar, is to wonder whether he will still be able to get to work on time. More recently, in Samuel Becket's plays, the characters peer anxiously from the ashcans or piles of sandy waste in which they are immobilized, exchanging trivial patter with each other. The promethean figure has vanished. His place has been taken by the milquetoast.

Correspondingly, the transgressor has become the hero. The saint is the insurrectionary. The Italian writer Ignazio Silone's protagonist in *Bread and Wine* is a hunted revolutionary who disguises himself as a priest. Treated as a priest by the villagers among whom he is hiding, he begins, to his own amazement, to think and act as one. He finds himself developing a new identity, one not too far from Silone's own description of himself as "a Christian without a church, a communist without a party." In our own country James Baldwin's writings bear a certain similarity to Silone's. Both are fascinated by the rebel saint. Silone finds Italian folk Catholicism constantly appearing in even his most revolutionary moments. Baldwin, who portrays the angry black hothead, constantly recurs to the imagery of the Negro church to give shape and coloration to his protest. Perhaps we should not be surprised by the unprecedented admixture of qualities appearing in the writings of these men. Arthur Koestler foresaw it when he wrote two decades ago that only a new mutation, a mixture of the saint and the revolutionary, would be able to save our age from destroying itself. In the literature and drama of our time this new saint is beginning to appear.

But the new styles of saintliness and sinnerhood are not restricted to the world of the imagination. Adolf Eichmann is a figure from our history, not from a play. As he appeared in his trial in Jerusalem Eichmann is the perfect embodiment of the twentieth-century sinner: an insipid sad-sack guilty of crimes so monstrous they defy the imagination. Many people remarked during the Eichmann trial that he made them feel uneasy because he looked so ordinary, so much like us. He sat in his glass cell polishing his spectacles and officiously correcting the punctuation marks on transcripts of testimony. Seemingly incapable of Luciferean evil, this human cipher was the man who committed genocide simply by doing what he was told, keeping his nose clean, and seeing to it that the trains ran on time.

But recent history has also produced its flesh-and-blood saints, and their lives stand out in vivid contrast to the pale, self-effacing saints of the religious goods stores. Wisely, the Catholic church has a policy of waiting decades or even centuries before canonizing someone a saint. This does not, however, prevent us from keeping a list of contemporary nominations. For many people such a list would surely include such people as Dorothy Day, Dietrich Bonhoeffer, Camilo Torres, and perhaps Martin Luther King. The list might also include Gandhi and some of the Buddhist monks and nuns who have immolated themselves to protest the destruction of Vietnam. Admittedly the latter are not Christians, but we should certainly have learned by now that one does not necessarily have to be a Christian to be a saint.

Notice that each of these people said yes to the summons to become a man of faith by becoming personally and painfully involved in the social struggle of his day. Each is in some way an insurrectionary. Dorothy Day cast her lot with the poor, against profits and property. Bonhoeffer took part in a plot to end the horror of World War II by assassinating Hitler, was arrested and garroted to death. Camilo Torres, the Colombian priest, summoned his fellow Christians to a revolutionary program for Latin America and was shot down in a skirmish between police and guerrillas. The new style saint is making his debut on the stage of real history not just in the pages of novels.

But does this emphasis on such exceptional people overlook the millions of unknown saints who quietly do their daily task with compassion and dedication? It should not, for there are such people and they are saints also. But the special exemplary cases do teach us something: that deference and passivity no longer provide the quintessence of sainthood. Protest, skepticism, anger, and even insubordination can also be expressions of obedience to the gospel. Likewise the traits of obedience, self-abnegation, docility, and forbearance can be expressions of sin.

I have already suggested that the venerable old term sloth describes our spiritual debility better than the word pride does. Sloth means being *less* than instead of *more* than man. Sloth describes our flaccid unwillingness to delight in the banquet of earth or to share the full measure of life's pain and responsibility. It means to abdicate in part or in whole the fullness of one's own humanity.

Sloth is admittedly an ugly word. In English it has come to mean indolence or laziness. It is the name given to an unattractive animal who likes to hang inertly from tree branches. Perhaps therefore we would do better to resurrect the Latin word *acedia* which is the word we try unsuccessfully to translate with sloth. *Acedia* comes from the Greek words not caring (*a*-not; *kedos*-care). The early Christian theologians considered *acedia* as one of the seven deadly sins (along with pride, covetousness, lust, anger, gluttony, and envy). Why then have we been so preoccupied with *pride* when we tried to describe human sin, while almost forgetting *acedia*?

For one thing we have pinpointed the "fall" of man too narrowly in the forbidden fruit story in Genesis. Recent biblical scholarship suggests that the whole first section of Genesis, not just the Adam and Eve story, must be taken into consideration in our investigation of human sin. The bludgeoning of Abel by Cain and the religious arrogance of the Tower of Babel also reveal facets of man's sin. Man constantly refuses to live in reciprocity with his fellow man, cultivating the fruits of the earth and having dominion over the beasts. He has a tendency to sell out.

However, let us take a second look at that incident in the garden, the first human sin. If we read that old story carefully, we will see it is not just a sin of pride. It is a sin of *acedia*. Eve shares with Adam the assignment of exercising mastery over all the creatures of the field. Her "original" misdeed was not eating the forbidden fruit at all. Before she reached for the fruit she had already surrendered her position of power and responsibility over one of the animals, the serpent, and let it tell her what to do. Thus self-doubt, hesitant anxiety, and dependency actually preceded that fatal nibble that has fascinated us for so long and made us fuse sin with pride. Adam and Eve are the biblical Everyman and Everywoman. Their sin is our sin. It is not promethean. We do not defy the gods by courageously stealing the fire from the celestial hearth, thus bringing benefit to man. Nothing so heroic. We fritter away our destiny by letting some snake tell us what to do.

Adam is the Everyman who at first will not and then cannot be man. But with the coming of the Second Adam, Christ, that changes. Here was man who would be and was a full man. In him the whole range of human responsibility is fully assumed again. He exercises the full prerogatives of manhood. He lives in vigorous give and take with thieves, priests, prostitutes, and little children. In the stories that Jesus spins, one of the most frequent characters is the steward, the man who must exercise the power assigned to him by the master. The cautious or irresponsible steward, the one who hides his money in the earth or beats the servants in the master's absence, reaps the rebuke of Jesus. The Apostle Paul also sees the life that God makes possible for man as that of an heir who, putting childhood dependencies firmly behind him, assumes the duties of an adult.

It is thus quite evident that images of timidity, abdication, and irresponsibility should figure just as prominently in a biblical doctrine of sin as do images of rebellion. Why then has our theological tradition concerned itself so obsessively with insubordination as the chief expression of sin?

Part of the answer can be given in the single word, politics. Theologies always develop within a particular political context. There is a political, or perhaps an ideological, factor that explains in part why images of protest and revolt became so central in the Christian doctrine of sin. With the conversion of Constantine, Christianity became the ruling ideology of the Empire. As such, one of its main functions was to provide the symbolic confirmation of imperial authority and thus to assure the maintenance of social order. It did so with noteworthy success for over a thousand years of relatively unified western European "Christian" civilization. It did so by deemphasizing sloth and accentuating pride as the worst form of sinfulness. Pride of course was equated with insubordination.

When the Reformation came, the magisterial reformers— Luther, Calvin, and the Anglicans—largely retained this emphasis. Since they had to rely too heavily on state power for carrying through their reforms, they necessarily preserved the dominant image of sinful man as disobedient, fractious, and insubordinate. There can be little doubt that the experience these reformers had with the more radical reformers—Muenzer, Servetus, the Levellers—encouraged the identification of piety with passivity in their own minds.

By the nineteenth century the merging of faith and docility had become so axiomatic that Kierkegaard, Marx, and Nietzsche had to become enemies of Christendom to make themselves heard. Each was condemned by the church but each was right in his own way. Kierkegaard taught that the only real sin was "the despairing refusal to be one's self"; Marx railed rightly against people who saw society as an eternal "given" rather than as something for which man himself is responsible. Nietzsche saw correctly that a vampire God who will not allow man to be a creator must be killed, and gladly performed the act of deicide himself. Each represents repentance from the sin of sloth at a different level. For Kierkegaard, and for those contemporary existentialists who are most influenced by him, the individual must choose his own identity and not allow himself to be named by the expectations others inflict upon him. For Marx, man had to discard his superstitious reverence for unjust social structures before he could begin to change them. Nietzsche hoped for a new man beyond the bourgeois clod of the nineteenth century, a man who would have the courage to shape the very symbols and meaning by which he would live in the world.

The sin against which these three nineteenth-century prophets preached is exactly what the word sloth, *acedia*, should convey. Sloth is one of the seven "deadly," or more correctly, "capital" sins. This doesn't just mean it is quantitatively worse, but that it is a "source sin," the kind of structural derangement from which other sins arise. As Roman Catholic theologian Joseph Pieper remarks, sloth does not mean mere idleness, as though hyperthyroid activism were its antidote; rather it means that man "renounces the claim implicit in his human dignity" (*Leisure, The Basis of Culture*, p. 38). In medieval terms this means that the slothful man does not will his own being, does not wish to be what he fundamentally and really is. This is why sloth is such a dangerously fertile sin. It tempts man to other expressions of inhumanity. It leads toward what we might today call estrangement.

As Kierkegaard, Marx, and Nietzsche saw, to be a man involves personal, social, and cultural initiative and innovation. It means accepting the terrifying duty of deciding who I will be rather than merely introjecting the stereotypes that others assign to me. It means opening my eyes to the way power is distributed and wielded in a society and assuming a full measure of the pain and temptation that goes with wielding it. It means defying any image of life that discourages criticism or undercuts human creativity. To be a man means to care for and love the fellow man Eve and with her to have dominion over the earth, to name and care for the creatures whom God places in the human world of freedom. To weasle out of any of these privileges is to commit the sin of *acedia*, to relapse into sloth.

All this suggests that apathy is the key form of sin in today's world. Apathy is one of the words Webster uses to define acedia. For Adam and Eve, apathy meant letting a snake tell them what to do. It meant abdicating what theologians have called the *gubernatio mundi*, the exercise of dominon and control over the world. For us it means allowing others to dictate the identities with which we live out our lives. Sartre's portrait of Jean Genet in *Saint Genet* depicts a man whose view of himself is totally dictated by the mean lusts and foul passions projected on him by others. The Jew, the Negro, the homosexual, and the hippy in our society have sometimes been forced to enact some of these roles for us. But in projecting our secret fears and fantasies onto them, we both impoverish ourselves and prostitute them. Man is that creature who is created to shape and enact his own destiny. Whenever he relinquishes that privilege to someone else, he ceases to be a man. It is precisely that Negro who takes off the Sambo costume, who stops playing the humiliating role whites have pasted together for him, who thus affirms the promise of the New Adam. His decision to be himself is an act of repentance from sloth.

But apathy is also, and perhaps mainly, a political trespass. It takes the form of hiding behind a specialty, a lack of knowledge, a fear of involvement, which become rationalizations for not assuming one's share in the responsible use of power in the world. Man's existence is by its very nature life with and for the fellow man. This makes it essentially political. The apathetic avoidance of politics is the sophisticated way in which we, like Cain, club our brothers to death. We abdicate our assignment as stewards in various ways. Whether it is the slumdweller who doesn't vote or picket or the MIT scientist who lets Washington decide what shall be done with the weapons systems he is designing, to slough off the political life is to fall into the deadly sin of *acedia* from which all sorts of lesser venial sins sprout and grow.

We must be careful today with all our emphasis on the servant role of the church not to give the impression that the gospel calls man to plebeian servility. It does not. It calls him to adult stewardship, to originality, inventiveness, and the governance of the world. Let's not let any snake tell us what to do.

# PART ONE

## ON NOT LEAVING IT TO THE SNAKE

# I

🔳

# The Death of God and the
# Future of Theology

🔳

IN ONE SENSE THERE IS NO FUTURE FOR THEOLOGY IN AN AGE OF THE "death of God," but in another sense we cannot be certain of this until we know what the phrase means and what the function of theology is. For "death of God" is sometimes used to mean different things, even by the same writer in a single paragraph. My own investigation has isolated three distinct meanings.

The first is *nonthestic or atheistic*. As Paul van Buren has said, "Christianity is about man and not about God." For van Buren it is futile to say anything at all about "God," since the word has no viable empirical referent. We must therefore construct some form of theology in which we stop talking about God. Religious devotion and even religious language may remain, but the referents are entirely changed.

Van Buren's methodology is borrowed from the rigorous techniques of British and American philosophical analysis. Another atheistic viewpoint is that of Thomas Altizer, who seems to be informed by certain Buddhist and Hegelian themes that have led him to assert that there once was a transcendent, real God, but that this God became immanent in Jesus and finally died in his crucifixion. In contrast to Van Buren, Altizer insists that we must not only use the word "God," but we must make the announcement of his death central to our proclamation today. He is not puzzled by the word; he not only knows what it means but is willing to say more about the history of God than most Christian theologies have said in the past. Furthermore, Altizer insists that "only the Christian can experience the death of God." Experiencing the death of God is, for Altizer, close to what has traditionally been associated with conversion.

The second sense in which the phrase "death of God" is used occurs in the context of *cultural analysis*. For Gabriel Vahanian, and sometimes William Hamilton, it simply means that the culturally conditioned ways in which people have experienced the holy have become eroded. Religious experience is learned in any culture just as other experience is learned, in the unspoken assumptions and attitudes which children absorb from their parents and from their closest environment. Our forebears learned from their forebears to expect the experience of the holy in socially defined ways, whether in the sunset, in a camp-meeting conversion or in holy communion. This experience was structured by a culture of residual Christendom, still bearing traces of what Paul Tillich calls "theonomy." But the coming of modern technology and massive urbanization shook the structures of traditional society and thereby dissipated the cultural ethos within which the holy had been experienced. Hence the "God" of Christendom is "dead." For most modern writers the phrase is metaphorical, but in a culture strongly influenced by pietism, where the reality of God is identified with the experience of God, the phrase may be taken literally as a somber and threatening event.

The third sense in which "God" is "dead" is one that I discussed in the last chapter of my book *The Secular City*, and it is in some respects similar both to Vahanian's and van Buren's viewpoints. For me, the idea of the "death of God" represents a *crisis in our religious language* and symbol structure, which makes the word "God" ambiguous. It is not that the word means nothing to "modern man," as van Buren contends, but that it means so many things to different people that it blurs communication rather than facilitates it.

For years the doctrine of God has been in trouble. Paul Tillich, who assailed the very idea that God "is" (in his *Systematic Theology*), would never have settled for an undialectical nontheism, although his attempt to move "beyond theism" (in *The Courage to Be*) probably contributed to the present situation in theology. Karl Barth's christological positivism may also have prepared the way. The "death-of-God" movement is an inheritance from them, dramatizing the bankruptcy of the categories we have been trying to use. It is more the symptom of a serious failure in theology than a contribution to the next phase.

Modes of religious experience are, as we have noted, shaped by cultural patterns. When social change jars the patterns, conventional ways of experiencing the holy disappear. When the thickly clotted symbol system of a preurban society is replaced by a highly differentiated and individuated urban culture, modalities of religious experience shift. When this happens gradually, over a long span of time, the religious symbols have a chance to become adapted to the new cultural pattern. The experience of the death of the gods, or of God, is a consequence of an abrupt transition which causes the traditional symbols to collapse, since they no longer illuminate the shifting social reality.

The "Death of God" syndrome can only occur where the controlling symbols of the culture have been more or less uncritically fused with the transcendent God. When a civilization collapses and its gods topple, theological speculation can move either toward a God whose being lies beyond culture (Augustine, Barth), toward some form of millenarianism, or toward a religious crisis that takes the form of the "death of God."

In our own period, which is marked by man's historical consciousness reaching out and encompassing everything in sight, the nooks and crannies formerly reserved for the transcendent have all been exposed. Pluralism and radical historicism have become our permanent companions. We know that all doctrines, ideals, institutions, and formulations, whether religious or secular, arise within history and must be understood in terms of their historical milieu. How then do we speak of a God who is somehow present in history, yet whose being is not exhausted by the limits of history? How, in short, do we maintain an affirmation of transcendence within the context of a culture whose mood is relentlessly immanentist? Perhaps a rediscovery of the millenarian tradition, a reappropriation of eschatology, is the way we must go. I will return to this shortly.

The crisis in our doctrine of God is a serious one. This cannot be denied. Nevertheless, our continued and correct insistence on the need to encounter God in *all* of life and not just in a "religious" or cultic precinct fails to express anything that really transcends "history," the source of our experiential reference for what we usually talk about. Some theologians, like Schubert M. Ogden, have responded to the present impasse by going back to the only significant constructive work that has been done in recent decades in American theology—the thought of Charles Hartshorne and Henry Nelson Wieman—and to the philosophy of Alfred North Whitehead. This tactic may eventually produce results, but so far it has not really resolved any of the radical criticisms raised by the "death-of-God" writers.

My own response to the dead-end signaled by the "death-of-God" mood is to continue to move away from any spatial symbolization of God and from all forms of metaphysical dualism. I am trying to edge cautiously toward a secular theology, a mode of thinking whose horizon is human history and whose idiom is "political" in the widest Aristotelian sense of that term, i.e., the context in which man becomes fully man.

As I move in this direction, there are certain traps I want to try to avoid. First, though it may be satisfactory for some, I want to steer clear of the mystical-atheistic monism of Thomas Altizer. From the perspective of the science of religion, mysticism and atheism have always been similar. Both lack the elements of encounter with an "Other," a confrontation that is characteristic of most forms of theism. In Altizer this structural similarity has come to explicit expression. Second, I want to avoid the uncritical empiricism of Paul van Buren. I think his methodological starting point, derived from contemporary British and American linguistic analysis, is too constrictive. It does not take sufficient account of the nonempirical functions of many modes of human speech, the open and changing character of all languages, and the place of any language within a larger universe of symbolic, metaphorical, and poetic modes of expression. Kenneth Burke, in *The Rhetoric of Religion*, has laid out a type of religious-language analysis which does embrace these larger cultural dimensions, thus offering a corrective to the analysts' presuppositions.

Finally, I want to steer clear of the inverse pietism of William Hamilton, whose perceptive analysis of the cultural mood [1] is sometimes confused with the theological task itself. Since he often deduces the temper of the culture from a description of his own moods and beliefs, the basis of his theology is extremely experiential. This may be good, especially in view of the unjustly severe disparaging of "experience" which was so characteristic of some followers of Karl Barth, but theology cannot become experiential in this sense without courting the danger of becoming subjective. Thus, while I can accept his diagnosis of the cultural *élan*, which is often correct, I decline to enlarge it into a properly theological claim.

Let me make it clear that I do not condemn the men I have just named. I do not wish to belittle their contributions. As Gordon Kaufman has suggested, many of us are engaged in different "experiments in thought," pushing ahead to think through the implications of this or that set of premises.[2] This theological diversity is a mark of strength, not of weakness. Let me make it clear, too, that if I regard undialectical religious

[1] See his essay "The New Optimism" in Hamilton and Altizer, *Radical Theology and the Death of God* (Indianapolis: Bobbs-Merrill, 1966).

[2] See Gordon D. Kaufman, "Theological Historicism as an Experiment in Thought" in *The Christian Century*, March 2, 1966, p. 268.

atheism as too easy a way out, I also find most available "theistic" options equally unattractive. The road ahead often seems narrow, dark, and perilous, yet we can neither retreat nor stand still. The best I can do now is to try to indicate where I hope a breakthrough might be found, to point in the direction I want to go, not to a spot where I have arrived.

For me, the way out of the "death-of-God" miasma which leads forward rather than backward is lighted, however flickeringly, by two of the seminal minds of our era, Pierre Teilhard de Chardin and Ernst Bloch. Both of these men are intellectual vagabonds; neither belongs to the theological club. But if our present decrepitude teaches us anything, it is that the club needs massive transfusions of new blood if it is to survive at all. I believe it is only by listening to such outsiders as these that any new health will come to the enterprise of theology.

Teilhard's theology is only accidentially scientific, in the narrow sense. It is really a Christian cosmology, the first that has really engaged the imagination of modern man. Teilhard correctly saw that for modern man the question of God would focus on the question of man. It inextricably coalesced with the issue of man's place in the enormously expanded world of modern science. Teilhard's complex theories about the role of centrifugal and centripetal forces in evolution, the new kind of heredity seen in man as a culture-bearing animal, and the crucial role man's consciousness of evolution will play in that evolution— these cannot be discussed here. The point they suggest, however, is that any contemporary thinking about God must begin with the recognition that man now sees himself as the one who can and must carry through many of the responsibilities which men of earlier millennia have assigned to their gods.

Between Teilhard, the maverick Catholic, and Bloch, the renegade Marxist, there are many differences; but one cannot help noticing the similarities. Both of them discuss transcendence in terms of the pressure exerted by the future on the present. Both see the future as that pressure on the present which is only possible where there is a creature who can orient himself toward the future and relate himself to reality by this orientation, in short a "creature who can hope." They both regard reality as a radically open-ended process. Teilhard detected in the logic of evolution an ever deepening humanization of man and "hominization" of the universe. Bloch concerned himself with "man-as-promise" and mapped out what he called "the ontology of the not-yet."

Teilhard's world of discourse was the breathtakingly massive universe and the appearance within it of the phenomenon of man, that point where the cosmos begins to think and to steer itself. Bloch's place of philosophizing is human history, released from its aboriginal timelessness and launched on a journey into the future by the "birth of the hope," an orientation introduced into the world by the biblical faith but now lost sight of by Christians. Both Bloch and Teilhard affirmed the centrality of what the Germans now call the *Impuls der Erwartung,* the impulse of expectancy. The one examined the way cosmic space and geological time seem to dwarf man, the other how history seems to buffet him. But neither became discouraged; both saw hope in man's growing capacity to apply science and critical reflection to the shaping of his own destiny.

We need a no-nonsense "leveling" in theological discourse. I think that if we can affirm anything real which also transcends history, it will be the future as it lives in man's imagination, nurtured by his memory and actualized by his responsiblity. Some theologians have already begun to explore the implications this would have for traditional ideas of eschatology and incarnation. Although I think Teilhard's legacy will increasingly help us in working out this new direction, it is Bloch who I believe will be more influential.

Bloch's massive book, *Das Prinzip der Hoffnung (The Principle of Hope),* first published in 1954, though difficult and often unclear, supplies the only serious alternative to Martin Heidegger's even more opaque *Sein und Zeit (Being and Time)* of 1927 as a philosophical partner for theology. Heidegger senses life to be hemmed in and radically finite but he still fiercely presses the desperate question of the *Sein des Seienden*, the meaning of the being of that which is. Heidegger's influence on modern theology has been enormous, but as I argued in *The Secular City*, it seems to me almost wholly deleterious. Bloch presses the same difficult questions that Heidegger raises, but he does so within an ontology that seeks to question and subvert the tight finitude of Heidegger's constricted human world.

Thus while Heidegger plumbs the caliginous depths of anxiety, care, and *Sein zum Tode* (being toward death), Bloch deals with that "infatuation with the possible" without which human existence is unthinkable. "The basic theme of philosophy," argues Bloch, "is that which is still not culminated, the still unpossessed homeland," and instead of anxiety and death "philosophy's basic categories should be 'frontier,' 'future,' 'the new' and the '*Traum nach vorwärts.*' " [3] Like Heidegger, Bloch considers himself to be an atheist. But just as many theologians, such as Rudolf Bultmann, Herbert Braun, and Heinrich Ott, have found ideas of worth in Heidegger, an atheist, so a new group has already begun to find promising hints in the works of Ernst Bloch. Thus Jürgen Moltmann's *Theologie der Hoffnung* [4] obviously owes much to Bloch, as does Gerhard Sauter's *Zukunft und Verheissung.* [5]

One point of continuing interest for the theologians is that Bloch not only engages in a brilliant analysis of man as "the creature who hopes," he also postulates a correspondence between *man* as the *hoping, dreaming being* and the *historical world itself.* He sees this correspondence (*Entsprechung*) between the "subjective of hope" and the "objectively possible," and he even tries (often unsuccessfully) to describe and elucidate it. The relationship between "subjective" and "objective" hope raises in Bloch's mind the question of an "identity" between

[3] Bloch, *Das Prinzip der Hoffnung* (Berlin: Suhrkampf Verlag, 1954), p. 83. Bloch's expression *Traum nach vorwärts* is simple enough German, but a literal translation would be "dream toward forward" rather than "dream toward the future," which is our closest idiomatic equivalent.

[4] München: Christian Kaiser Verlag, 1964; ET, *Theology of Hope*, London: SCM Press, 1967.

[5] Zurich: Zwingli Verlag, 1965.

man-who-hopes and a structure of reality which supports and nourishes such hope.

Here the Christian naturally thinks of qualities sometimes attributed to God. Bloch is not unaware of the similarity; indeed he describes the identity between subjective spontaneity and historical possibility as the "demythologized content of that which Christians have revered as God." He therefore insists that atheism is the only acceptable stance today because the Christian God has been imprisoned in the categories of a static ontology.

There are many questions to be asked about Bloch's work from a biblical perspective. He does not provide us with a clear-cut way out of the "death-of-God" morass. At many points in his argument Bloch's commitment to radical historicism, along with residual traces of his Marxist materialism, seems to collide with his passionate desire to picture a radically open world in which at least the possibility of something "wholly other" is not excluded in principle. There are several places where, for example, he insists that all possibility is already incipiently present in what is, thus betraying an Aristotelian teleological bias. But his main thesis cannot be easily dismissed.

I agree with Wolf-Dieter Marsch's remark that as long as Christians cling to the static "is" as the normative predicate for God, such thinkers as Bloch must rightly continue to regard themselves as atheists. But if theology can leave behind the God who "is" and begin its work with the God who "will be" (or in biblical parlance "He who comes"), an exciting new epoch in theology could begin, one in which Ernst Bloch's work would be extraordinarily important.

If the present wake is for the God who *is* (and now *was*), this may clear the decks for the God who *will be*. No one can say for sure that the opening of such a path will lead anywhere, but the task of opening it would first require a thorough reworking of our major theological categories. We would see Jesus, for example, not as a visitor to earth from some supraterrestrial heaven, but as the one in whom precisely this two-story dualism is abolished for good, and who becomes the pioneer and first

sign of the coming New Age. We would see the community of
faith as those "on the way" to this promised reality, "forgetting
what is behind and reaching out for that which is ahead" (Phil.
3:14). Radical theology would have more radical social consequences than the so-called radical theology of the death of God
has produced so far.

The doctrine of God would become theology's answer to the
seemingly irrefutable fact that history can only be kept open by
"anchoring" that openness somewhere outside history itself,
in this case not "above" but *ahead*. Faith in God would be recognized, for our time, in that hope for the future Kingdom of Peace
that frees men to suffer and sacrifice meaningfully in the present.
It would be premature and maybe even a little glib to pretend that
in the God of Hope we can immediately affirm the one who will
appear when the corpse of the dead God of metaphysical theism
is finally interred. He may not appear at all, and our efforts to
work out a new and viable doctrine of God for our time may
be fated to fail from the beginning. But before any of us throws
in the towel, I hope we will exercise the freedom given us by
the present *Götterdämmerung* of the divinities of Christendom,
and use the freedom to think as candidly and as rigorously as
possible about where we go from here.[6]

The only future that theology has, one might say, is to become
the theology of the future. Its attention must turn to that future
which God makes possible but for which man is inescapably
responsible. Traditionally, it is prophecy that has dealt with the
future. Hence the fate of theology will be determined by its
capacity to regain its prophetic role. It must resist the temptation
of becoming an esoteric specialty and resume its role as critic
and helper of the faithful community as that community grapples
with the vexing issues of our day.

The "death-of-God" syndrome signals the collapse of the static

[6] Since writing this article I have read Leslie Dewart's engaging new book,
*The Future of Belief: Theism in a World Come of Age* (London: Burns &
Oates, 1967). It is a suggestive example of a new possibility in theism once we
have divested ourselves of static metaphysical categories. Dewart stresses the
"presence" rather than the existence of God.

orders and fixed categories by which men have understood themselves in the past. It opens the future in a new and radical way. Prophecy calls man to move into this future with a confidence informed by the tradition but transformed by the present. Theology helps prophecy guide the community of faith in its proper role as the avant-garde of humanity. This community must clarify the life-and-death options open to *homo sapiens*, devote itself unsparingly to the humanization of city and cosmos, and keep alive the hope of a kingdom of racial equality, peace among the nations, and bread for all. One should never weep for a dead god. A god who can die deserves no tears. Rather we should rejoice that, freed of another incubus, we now take up the task of fashioning a future made possible not by anything that "is" but by "He who comes."

## II

⊞

# The Place and Purpose
# of Theology

⊞

THE ISSUE OF WHAT THEOLOGY IS IS ITSELF A THEOLOGICAL ISSUE.
It concerns the *place* and *purpose* of theologizing. It includes such
considerations as what a "theological problem" is and how and
where theological issues arise. *What* we think is determined far
more than we realize by *where* we think (our *"Sitz im Denken"*)
and *why* we think (the *aim* of theological inquiry). I would argue
that the purpose of theology is to serve the prophetic community.
For this reason the place of theology is that jagged edge where the
faithful company grapples with the swiftest currents of the age.
Any "theology" which occurs somewhere else or for some other
reason scarcely deserves the name.

We all sense that there is something wrong in theology.
To nurse our calling back to health, it is our task as theologians
to enlist it again in the service of prophecy. This means we must
stand between two determinative clusters of events: the demise of

religion as an unquestioned cultural ethos and the emergence of revolution as the decisive form of the new world civilization.

The task of prophecy is to illuminate contemporary history, to clarify the crucial options and to summon man to the responsible stewardship of his world. The task of theology is to guide, criticize, and deepen prophecy. But theology is sick. Its dyspepsia and delirium arise mainly from the fact that theology is preoccupied with religion, either morbidly or stubbornly, and that it still exhibits insufficient interest in discerning the signs of the times— in revolution. Rather than helping the prophets greet a revolutionary tomorrow, we theologians are more interested in dissecting the cadaver of yesterday's pieties. Instead of scanning the temporal horizon for signs of the new humanity, many of us flee from the bewildering secular matrix where this promised community is taking shape. We repair to the religious ghetto either by devoting our talents to the defense of "God" or by staring in hypnotic fascination at the oblong cavity left by his presumed expiration.

The opponents in the current sham battle over whether the deity is dead or alive seem at first to be on opposite ends of the spectrum. In reality, however, they stand quite close together. They represent two interdependent responses to the collapse of the "religious phase" of theology's career in Western culture. One tries to resuscitate the god of religion; the other seeks to fashion a new kerygma around his disappearance. Both seem somehow nineteenth century in style. To move fully into the twentieth century theology must free itself of two paralyzing prejudices which have tended, especially in recent years, to divert it from its proper prophetic role.

I

The first bias I call the *ecclesiastical* bias. It has affected us mainly in our view of the history of theology and of the prophetic community within which it stands. We have tended in our histories of doctrine to assign most weight to those movements and

B

personages that have left some visible ecclesiastical residue: a creed, a sect, a church. We devote 100 pages to Luther and three lines to Münzer. But why? Karl Mannheim believes the social revolutions of the sixteenth century, for which Münzer was a leader and theoretician, unleashed tides which still move our world today, albeit in secular form. Yet Luther gets our attention not just because his princes defeated the Peasant uprising (Münzer was beheaded) but because he endowed a church and a religious movement with his name.

Our attention to the seventeenth century focuses mainly on the emergence of the Presbyterian and free churches in Britain. They are the ecclesiastical forebears of many of our American churches. But the most important contribution of the Puritans, as Michael Walzer has shown in his brilliant book *The Revolution of the Saints* (Cambridge, Mass: Harvard University Press, 1965), may not be churches at all but the fact that they originated the politics of participatory democracy. As the critical tracts of the Cavaliers tauntingly reported, in Cromwell's army "even cobblers and tinkers" were exhorted to political discussion and action. Our ecclesiasticized reading of history, by which the British Labor party becomes merely a side effect of the Wesleyan revivals, is no more than prejudice. But it numbs our senses and complicates the task of guiding prophecy today. It makes theologians too religious. It leads them to believe that politics can be only a secondary interest. This prejudice comports well with Richard Hooker, but it misses any connection with Amos.

History, the Marxists say, is written by the victors. Theological history is written by ecclesiastical chroniclers whose well-intentioned portrait of where we have come from blinds us to our present task—discerning the evidences of the Kingdom in the secular turmoil of the times. Prophecy demands a right reading of history. We must begin as theologians to make up our minds not in the light of ecclesiastical or religious history alone but in the light of all of history, viewed as the record of man's response, often in secular and antireligious ways, to the summons and surprise of the gospel.

## II

The *existentialist* bias also holds us in its grip. It especially
effects those of us who work in systematic or hermeneutical theology. It has hexed us into a fascination with what Helmut Gollwitzer calls "the abstract Ego," confronted constantly by desperate
decisions, called to constitute its selfhood by a towering act of
will. The world, the society, history, and the revolution—all fade
into secondary significance as the isolated Ego reacts to the dis-
embodied Word.

Admittedly I caricature. There is in authentic existentialism a
kind of giddy grandeur, even though many of its Christian versions, especially in America, sound too much like sophisticated
revivalism. But existentialism is merely the philosophical shadow
of the crisis in religion. Religious existentialism was bound to
deteriorate eventually into just the melodramatic Spenglerian apocalypticism it has reached in its current phase, the maudlin
celebration of the demise of deity.

But the witches' sabbath needs the conventional Sunday, and
the black mass makes no sense without the orthodox one. Live
God and Dead God theologies need each other to beat on, like
Punch and Judy. But their common problem is that both are very
"religious" in the worst sense of the word, i.e., occult, apolitical,
and esoteric.

We need a prophetic stance in theology. We need to focus
the vision of the biblical tradition, on those secular epiphanies
where the new man and the new society are bursting forth in the
thick of today's sexual, literary, racial, and economic transforma-
tions. We need a prophecy, and therefore a theology that is political in this grandly inclusive sense, i.e., focusing on the *polis*, the
milieu where man becomes man. How do we start making up our
minds in a political not just a religious context?

We start on one side by repairing the breech between the Old
and New Testaments, and their respective communities of faith.
As Hans Wolff correctly charges, "Our New Testament theology
is largely only half true because it fails to recognize the historical

bonds that tie it to the Old Testament. These bonds are much more decisive than those which tie it to the Judaism or Hellenism of its day."

The first schism in the church, the one between Christianity and Israel, remains the most serious and destructive one. It dissipated our feel for the gritty historicity of Israel's faith and encased us in the timeless categories of Hellenistic metaphysics.

The Old Testament is not a very religious book, as Kornelis Miskotte shows in his important work *Wenn die Götter schweigen* (*When the Gods Are Silent*, ET London: Collins, 1967). If we stood closer to the Old Testament—and this means closer to the spiritual descendants of Israel, the so-called "religious" as well as the so-called "nonreligious" Jews—we would have a better locus for making up our minds theologically.

The link between the church and Israel is Jesus of Nazareth, and the fault for making him more of a barrier than a bridge lies mainly on the Christian side. We need as our theological starting point a Jesus who is neither the ecclesiastical nor the existentialist Jesus, nor the Jesus toward whom the church has developed a downright proprietary attitude, but the Jewish Jesus. Our Christology must begin with the Jew who makes it possible for us to share the hope of Israel, the hope for a Kingdom of Shalom. Christians, as Krister Stendahl rightly says, are really only honorary Jews. All Jesus does for Israel's hope is to universalize it, to make it available even to us goyim. But the church has betrayed his gift. Instead of universalizing the hope, we have etherealized it. It has become a fond wish for something after, beyond or above this earth or for something within the self. In Christianity the hope of Israel has almost ceased to be a lively hope for the *world*.

Cut off from a universal dimension, the hope of Israel itself, although it is still worldly, has become provincial and sometimes even nationalistic. Only when the hope of Israel and the Church are fused does a hope which is both universal and secular appear. As Jürgen Moltmann says, we must think theologically on the basis of hope: *Spero ut intelligam*. It is the Judaeo-Christian hope which must illuminate theology today.

But we also live in a second schism which also distorts our theology. The failure of our theology to nurture a hope for this world led to the schism now separating the church from movements devoted to social change and human justice. Whereas the first schism makes it hard for theology to give up *religion*, either ecclesiastical or existentialist, the second schism prevents us from coming to terms with *revolution*. This is extremely ironic, for revolution, as Rosenstock-Huessy has shown, is a Western phenomenon with its roots in biblical faith. Yet, because of the church's proclivity for alliances with the establishments, the great revolutions of the West, beginning with the peasants revolt and climaxing with the Russian revolution, have become progressively more anti-Christian. Finding little hospitality within the church, this hope for a new world which originated with the gospel, as the Marxist Ernst Bloch has documented, migrated out into secular revolutionary movements. They are its legitimate heirs, cut off from the criticism and support of the church.

Just as the separation of the church from Israel blurs the vision of both, thus deforming theological thinking, so this second schism vitiates the health and distorts the perception of both Christians and revolutionary alike. The ruination of revolutionary movements is that, shorn of truly universal scope, they degenerate into narrow vendettas exploited by cynical elite groups. The thrilling slogan of 1787, "Liberté, égalité, fraternité," is debauched in Napoleonic gore. The humanistic ideals of communism disappear in the Stalinist humiliation of Ivan Denisovich.

### III

Yet if the great movements for social change, originating in the West and now spreading around the world, are heretical versions of the Christian hope, then the version of that hope espoused by the churches is equally heretical. While the hope of revolutionaries often becomes narrow or jingoistic, the hope of the church becomes interior or extraterrastrial. The end result of the first is thermidor; of the second, legitimism. Both spell reaction.

How then do we close the schism between the church and the movements for social change, thus eliminating another cause of our present theological astigmatism? Again I think the figure of Jesus provides the key. In him we catch a glimpse of the possibilities of man and history. Economist Robert Heilbroner in his suggestive book *The Future as History* argues that our characteristically modern and Western belief that we *can* accomplish historical change "does not ultimately rest on a judgment about our historic capacities" but rather on the "tacit premise that the future will accommodate the striving we bring to it. It is based on the faith that the historic environment . . . will prove benign and congenial."

The prophetic community finds in Jesus, and in the whole movement which culminates in him, a clue to the character of what Heilbronner calls "the historic environment." It links him with the prototypical man as the New Adam and sees in him a new chance to shoulder the responsibility the old Adam betrayed. In tending the garden, naming the creatures, and subduing the earth we see a secular assignment necessitating choice, venture, and the wielding of power. It links him also with the leader of a social revolution as the New Moses and finds that political oppression and economic serfdom must be left behind if we are to push toward a promised future. Does it seem too obsolete to suggest that even for theologians "following Jesus" is a necessary prerequisite to right *thinking* about him? Or that "following Jesus" will inevitably make us participants and not just onlookers in today's social revolution? Theology detached from discipleship, theology outside the prophetic fellowship, becomes barren. To follow Jesus means to be on the move, to abandon old formulations when they no longer serve, to address new issues as they appear.

The theologian who is not making up his mind at the place where today's new Adams and new Moseses are composing new chapters in the biblical saga is out of place; the purpose he serves is spurious; and his theology will continue to be chimerical and apolitical. Consequently it will not be prophetic. The issues he tackles will be the acrostic puzzles of academia, not the life-and-death questions of men of faith in a world of change.

What is our place and purpose as theologians today? We must try to stand with one foot in the discordant history of Israel, old and new, and the other foot in the convulsive habitat of the frankly profane man of our late twentieth century. This teetery platform provides our *place*. We stand there trying to hear and to help our comrades in the cadre of prophets, as together we discern the traces and sometimes drink the wines of the coming new era.

# III

✦

# The Gospel and
# Postliterate Man

✦

Hermeneutics—the problem of interpreting past truth for the present day—is regarded by Gerhard Ebeling and others as the key theological issue of our time. The problem has two foci: the essential message to be transmitted and the situation of the "man of today" for whom the message is intended. Theologians disagree about both points, but perhaps the more violent argument rages around that elusive character the "man of today." What is his nature? Is he already somehow "beyond religion" (as seen by Bonhoeffer), is he still "religious in his subconscious" (as seen by Eliade) or does he ask religious questions in nonreligious garb (in accordance with Tillich's view)? Or is he, as Barth would contend, in no way essentially different from his ancestors?

## I

In probing this crucial issue theologians tend to overlook one modern development which could render the whole discussion obsolete. They forget the appearance in our time of what Marshall

McLuhan calls "postliterate man." If McLuhan is right, we could be entering an epoch in which man's perception of God, self, and world will be more markedly altered than even the most radical modern theologian can appreciate. The replacement of book-and-print culture with a vision of reality arising from the grammar and metaphor characteristic of the electronic image could bring about immeasurably significant changes for our entire culture, for theology, and especially for hermeneutics. It could call into question assumptions which have governed our thinking since the invention of writing. As McLuhan says: "The Age of Writing has passed. We must invent a New Metaphor, restructure our thoughts and feelings." The change in our mode of experiencing reality would be comparable to that which occurred when the development of the art of writing made it possible for man to record his history. Such a modification in the fundamental fabric of human existence would raise theological questions more far-reaching than any we have touched so far. But first we must ask: Is the communications revolution really that radical?

Many serious students of the relation between culture and communication believe it may be. McLuhan is now professor at Fordham University. His books have always sparked lively controversy. His style sometimes jars and angers readers, but he cannot be dismissed simply as an oddball. Along with anthropologist Edmund Carpenter, literary critic Stanley Edward Hyman, Gilbert Seldes of the University of Pennsylvania's Annenburg School of Communications, and others, he contributed to *Explorations*, a lively journal published 1953-59.

It is not now possible to schematize the seminal thinking of this interdisciplinary group, but its general contention is clear: that when the technology of communications media changes there is a concomitant change in the culture's way of perceiving reality. Various communications technologies entail varying "codifications of reality." For example, book-and-print cultures do not simply see, through a new medium, the same world preliterate man saw; they perceive a new reality. Both the view of the world and the experience of the self are wholly transformed by the development of new communications techniques. With the coming of writing, men changed their way of perceiving space and time. They put aside the cyclical categories of myth and adopted a linear perspective which comported with the parade of script characters across a surface. This change, McLuhan and his group hold, signaled sweeping religious and social metamorphoses of which we should be more cognizant. For McLuhan, however, the essential point is that today we are living through a period of similar decisiveness. The visual electronic image has begun to displace the written word as our main communications medium. He believes that we are witnessing the birth of "postliterate man," a creature whose identity image and world view will differ as widely from ours as our life style differs from that of preliterate tribal cultures.

All this may sound a bit far-fetched. But the skeptics who shrug off this argument are precisely those whose perceptive stance McLuhan and his colleagues have called into question. They are readers, denizens of the passing book-and-print period. The fact that for most of us the printed page provides our key to vast ranges of social reality tends to make us ineligible to evaluate the importance of the electronic image. But an increasing number of people see the world in a different light. Our generation read or heard about most things before we saw them; now through television our children see things first and later learn to read about them. With the spread of movies and television to Africa and Asia millions of adults are leapfrogging from the preliterate to the postliterate age without traversing the intervening stage. For many people in our country the television screen has become the main source of awareness of the political and economic world beyond their own experience, with newspapers and books playing a subsidiary role. This is not to suggest that postliterate man cannot read. He may be able to read, just as literate man can hear stories and songs, but reading no longer provides his basic orientation to reality. His primary perception has been determined by the logic of the electronic image.

## II

For example, let us examine the implications of the communications revolution in the contrast between reading a novel (still a familiar activity) and watching a movie (its rough equivalent for postliterate man). The most obvious difference is that one does not have to learn to watch a movie. The experience carries with it no need to master a language or even to learn to read one's own language. Also, while book reading begins with a rational-intellectual process (i.e., decoding certain marks on a paper) and *may* lead toward emotional involvement, the experience of watching a movie is characterized by the reverse: the viewer is exposed to a more direct and immediate experience which may possibly give rise to intellectual response.

However, there is an even more important difference. The reader holds the book in his own hands, can look up from it, close it, or hurl it into the fireplace, but the movie watcher has no such control over the film. If he looks away, it flickers on. If he misses a point, he cannot check back. If he becomes annoyed he can hiss or boo, though at the risk of being reprimanded, and if he is really angry he can only stumble through the dark aisles and leave the theater. Reading is generally a solitary activity carried on in the privacy of one's home. Attending a movie is freqeuntly a group undertaking carried on outside the home, at the cost of an admission fee. David Riesman suggests concerning the psychological correlate of reading: "The book, like the door, is an encouragement to isolation. . . . It helps liberate the reader from the group and its emotions, and allows the contemplation of alternative responses." The movie has almost the opposite effect. The viewer is with a group but he is alone in the crowd. Although he may be accompanied by family or friends it is necessary for him to remain silent and to communicate through shared emotions rather than through rational conversation. He may discuss the film later, but the important elements of critical distance and rational control play a role of lesser importance than in reading. We turn *on* the lights to read but to see a movie we turn them *off*, or—and perhaps this is more significant—someone else does.

## III

According to the new communications theorists, the change of medium in the transition from book to film culture entails a far more important change in world view, with alterations in the primal perception of reality. The postliterate man, as contrasted to the book reader, lives in a world which is directly present for him and to which he tends to respond with similar immediacy. He perceives the world without the feeling of critical control the book reader develops. Although the physical conditions under which he watches television are more conducive to criticism and conversation, the impossibility of reobservation by flipping back a page is a critical factor. This leads to discussion of impressions and reactions with others. Thus, as watching television programs and films is often a group undertaking, criticism of those media is also a social activity.

The deep relevance of this discussion for Protestants lies in the fact that Protestantism is par excellence the religion of the Book. It arose with the development of printing, was characterized by its insistence on the believer's right to peruse the Scriptures, and spread around the world on the wings of tractarian movements, colporteurs, literacy campaigns, and Bible societies. Perhaps the classical image of Protestant man is one of the individual believer, seated alone with his Bible, reverently but critically reading, marking, and being conditioned by it. Puritanism's tendency toward individualism, its support of the privilege of private opinion and its traditional suspicion of emotional involvement and visual images cohere with the politics and psychology of the book-and-print era. If McLuhan and his group are even partially correct in their analysis of the communications revolution, what does this mean for the future of Protestant man?

In considering this question we should not forget that though the Reformers stressed the Bible and the preached Word they were not unaware of the visual components of existence. Luther called the sacraments the *verba visibilia*, the "visible words," and early Baptists, immersing new converts in rivers, recognized the public impact of a dramatic reenactment of the believer's participation in the death and ressurection of Jesus. Although the Reformation set loose some iconoclastic currents it also produced Rembrandt.

## IV

Yet Roman Catholicism makes greater use of visual media. The medieval church was lavishly visual, from the cathedrals themselves with their stained glass and statuary to the vestments and movements of the mass. A mass on television today is visually more interesting than a Protestant service centered in pulpit and preaching.

But the issue of postliterate man has more than merely technical inferences: it poses profound theological questions. McLuhan argues, for example, that the linear sense of time is part of the metaphysics of books and print. He could have strengthened his case by a reference to Augustine, whose meditations on the mystery of time began while he was reading a Psalm, glancing occasionally at the preceding and forthcoming verses, or to Luther, whose liberating discovery that God had already forgiven him came as he meditated on the text of Romans. Some historians have suggested that it was really Christians who invented bookbinding: they preferred the book to the scroll because with the book they could check one passage against another.

But there are limits to McLuhan's insight. At times he even goes so far as to suggest that with the electronic image we will return to a tribal culture in which a "simultaneous-cluster" view of time will replace the one-directional arrow. Surely he is mistaken about this. Our present hardening of lineal time into a strict mechanical sequence will probably not survive the electronic era. But after experiencing lineal time we can not return completely to the mythical perspective. We will evolve a new concept of time which, while directional, will allow for the intensity, pace, and flexibility which characterize visual media.

The most important result we can expect is this: that the visible *style* of the church's life will become a much more significant element in the communication of the gospel. This does not mean a return to an arid ritualism. It means that the church itself may become the *verbum visibile*, the visual enactment of the message it bears, in a newly important way. This is why present discussion of the "shape" of the church is so significant. In a culture increasingly dependent on visual parables and signs for its orientation to the world, the conduct of the Christian community, its visible behavior, will become a much more significant "word" than the pronouncements of the pulpit.

# PART TWO

## DON'T DIE IN THE WAITING ROOM

# IV

⊠

## Tradition and Future:
## The Need for New Perspective

---

⊠

ONE OF THE MOST ARRESTING FEATURES OF THE MENTALITY OF THE
late twentieth century is its preoccupation with the future. Planning, forecasting, extrapolation, and various forms of computerized
soothsaying have begun to provide a new frame of reference for
politics and even for philosophy. Utopianism is no longer a mortal
sin and to call someone visionary does not mean he can be dismissed without further consideration. Marxists use the future the
way a previous generation used the providence of God: to awake
people from sloth and slumber, to speed missionaries to unen-
lightened lands, to harness disciplined work forces, and to post-
pone immediate gratification in the interests of the hereafter.
Economic planners tell us that an underdeveloped country turns a
crucial corner when its leaders begin to think not of next week
and next month, but of next year and the next decade.

Our interest in the future has spawned a bevy of conferences,
research centers, and institutes. Robert Jungk's Institute für Zuk-
unft-sfragen in Vienna and Bertrand de Jouvenal's "Futuribles" try
to peer into the coming unknown and refine the methods of

prognostication. Herman Kahn pens his technicolor scenarios at the Hudson Institute. The American Academy of Arts and Sciences appointed a "Commission on the Year 2000" to prepare a recent issue of its magazine *Daedalus*.

Naturally there are many questions to be raised about such a precarious business, what its methodology should be, how projections can be checked against others. I wish however to raise some of the philosophical and even theological questions involved in this emerging mood of future orientation. It will be my contention that a serious effort to think systematically about the future and to hold the future open for man will eventually stretch some of our existing canons of thought to the snapping point. But this enterprise may also result in a valuable rediscovery of certain neglected elements in the biblical heritage. It will prove beneficial, however, only if we go into it fully conscious of the colossal challenge it represents to many of our accepted ways of thinking and only if we become aware of the historical roots of this present effort to make the future rather than the past normative for social ethics and political theory.

Reinhold Niebuhr gave much thought to the future as a theological problem. His chapters on messianism in *The Nature and Destiny of Man* are still fresh and readable today. Still his main contribution was on another point. He gave depth to the critique of the philosophical assumptions underlying political liberalism by grounding the critique in the moral tradition of the Hebrew prophets, Augustine, and the Reformers. But in order to provide such a grounding Niebuhr first had to extricate this tradition from its admixture with romantic, Enlightenment, and nineteenth-century progress views of man and history. In other words his task was twofold: first to purify an older and more comprehensive tradition from motifs with which it had combined in its more recent history; then to show how this tradition could provide an ethos that would affect political decision-making.

Our task today again has these two stages: reconstituting the moral tradition by pruning and purification; then indicating how this perspective can illuminate present political quandaries. Niebuhr's separation of the biblical tradition from certain motifs of Enlightenment and classical liberal worldviews came as a shock to many. These components had cohabited for so long they often looked not like a conglomerate but like a permanent and irreducible synthesis. Still they were separated out, to the significant enrichment of the universe of discourse within which decisions were made.

Nonetheless, Niebuhr's separation may seem simple in comparison to the one our generation must undertake. We are challenged today not just to separate biblical motifs from comparatively recent cultural additives but to separate the Hebrew from the Hellenistic constituent of the whole Western Christian tradition. This is not a recent synthesis, but one that dates from the earliest centuries of Christianity. It informs not just liberal Christianity, which is after all only a relatively modern and even somewhat provincial expression of the tradition, but forms the very thought categories within which theology and much of Western philosophy have operated. This synthesis of Hebrew prophetism with late Greek philosophy was spread around the ancient world and transmitted into the medieval world by Christianity. It provided the thought forms with which the Western moral tradition has proceeded for nearly two millenia. Occasionally one or another of the components will receive heavier emphasis: the Greek during the Renaissance, the Hebrew in the Reformation, the Greek again in the Enlightenment, the Hebrew in Marxism. Still, the categories within which this dynamic altercation has gone on stem from the synthesis which now stands in question. It may be the dissolution of this old synthesis which gives our period some of its malaise and *fin de siècle* mentality. Since the term "God" has functioned as the central symbol of this system, the "God-is-dead" thinking is also a reflection of its dissolution.

Why is this venerable theological tradition now in question? The simplest answer is that any symbol system becomes dysfunctional when it no longer provides an adequate horizon of perception, thinking, and acting. In a relatively stable society, where the main task of the moral philosopher was to relate past to present, the Hebrew-Hellenistic synthesis was a viable one. Now, however, our fascination with the future, our permanent crisis mentality, and our deep conciousness of change grate against the Hellenistic component of this tradition; the synthesis becomes increasingly impossible to maintain. Niebuhr saw behind the modern biblical-liberal synthesis to the more basic problem of this Hebrew-Hellenistic synthesis, but he did not go far enough in separating the one from the other. In our period, however, this task has moved to the top of the agenda. Why? Stated quite simply it is this: our task is to make sense out of the future, to develop an attitude toward it which is appropriate to its character. The Greeks, however, had no future; for the Hebrews, the future was everything. If Niebuhr's accomplishment was to extricate and show the relevance of the Judaeo-Christian view of man for politics, our challenge is to extricate the characteristically Hebrew dimension of this tradition and to show how it informs an open and responsible view of the future.

It is important here to clarify the difference between the Greek and Hebrew views of the future. In a real sense the Greeks did not believe in a historical future. The basic concept for them was "being," and being was characterized by an eternally changeless character. Plato's ideas are immortal and invariable. Men are born, struggle, and die, but what appears to be change really amounts only to transient approximations of the eternal or the endless repetition of cycles within a horizon of nonhistorical being. There is no genuine future.

Greek philosophy and its Hellenistic derivatives grow out of Greek religion, which was itself simply the sophisticated descendent of a cosmological, nature-oriented religious system. The lack of real historical consciousness in this type of religion is brilliantly described in Mircea Eliade's book *The Myth of Eternal Return*. For all its power and sublimity, still the idea of eternal return excludes the possibility of an authentic historical future.

For the Hebrews on the other hand, the world itself *was* history. God's word to man, his *dabar*, was a promise that directed man toward a future in which this promise would be fulfilled. It was a promise of land, of national restoration, of a new era. These promises were constantly frustrated and disappointed. But God always promised something else and the future was open again. The covenant community was made up of those people to whom the promise had been given and who would be included in its fulfillment. The highest expression of this religion of promise was the hope for a universal messianic era in which all enmity would be abolished and the nations would be united in peace and justice.

This throbbing Hebrew sense of future expectation was not throttled by the coming of Christianity. True, the early church preached that in Jesus the long awaited messiah had come. But it also proclaimed that his Kingdom of peace and justice, though inaugurated, had yet to be fulfilled. The crucified messiah was still in some sense alive and would appear again to make fully visible a kingdom that was now hidden and incomplete. Thus early Christianity was also extremely future oriented. But this open and expectant attitude toward the future in early Christianity was tempered by two influences. One was dualistic *apocalypticism*; the other was Greek *teleology*.

Hebrew religion had reached a kind of impasse in its eschatology just before the beginning of the Christian era. Some rabbis taught that the messianic era would come on earth and in history. Others influenced by Persian motifs believed that it would come only in a blazing end to the present historical era. Christianity inherited from Israel both these eschatological traditions and never combined them with complete success. At times the New Testament seems to say that the coming Kingdom of God will transform and renew this earth. At other times this earth seems to be swallowed up in flames while a whole new and pristine world appears. The orthodox doctrine of the Trinity, which taught that God who had created the world and the God who was renewing it were one and the same mitigated against a purely negative, antiworldly apocalypticism. And so did the decision of the early churches to retain the Hebrew scriptures, with their blatant earthiness, as an integral element of the Bible. Christian theology thus escaped the temptation of becoming one more *apocalyptic*, world-denying cult.

But no sooner had this battle been won then Christianity was faced with a new crisis from which it has still not sufficiently recovered. When it moved from Palestine into the Hellenistic culture of the Mediterranean basin, it had to adapt itself to the prevailing thought system of its day or be written off as just another provincial Jewish sect. Christian theologians did so by embracing Hellenistic philosophy, including a *teleological* view of history. The resulting mixture of late Hellenism and Hebrewism provided the intellectual basis for the entire history of the west. God became the *ens*, being itself, and his attributes were those of changelessness, aseity, and eternality. Centuries of theological battles were fought over how Jesus could have been divine yet still have lived in history, suffered pain, and died. Theologians thought out elaborate schemes about two natures united in one person to answer this problem. Even today, we still move within assumptions and modes of thought laid down in this astounding cultural synthesis.

Thus we inherit from Christianity three different, even contradictory, ways of perceiving the future. The *apocalyptic*, deriving from ancient near Eastern dualism, foresees imminent catastrophe, produces a negative evaluation of this world, and often believes in an elite which will be snatched from the inferno when everything else dissolves. *Teleology*, derived mainly from the Greeks but adapted by Christianity, sees the future as the unwinding of a purpose inherent in the universe itself or in its primal stuff, the development of the world toward a fixed end. The *prophetic* is the characteristically Hebrew notion of the future as the open field of human hope and responsibility. The Israelite prophets did not, as many popular misconceptions would have it, "foretell the future." They recalled Yahweh's promise as a way of calling the Israelites into moral action in the present.

During the long millenium in which a "politics of the future" was not the major preoccupation of the west, this unstable compound could stay together. Indeed at those points where there were moments of intense fascination with the future, such as with Joachim of Fiore (1132–1202), and in millenarian and chiliastic groups, the synthesis was threatened. Today, however, orientation toward the future is not a minority preoccupation but the mood of a whole culture. Hence, the contradictions in the tradition become more noticeable, hastening the dissolution of the compound.

As societies become secularized, the values they once produced and nurtured often continue to function long after the symbolic grounding of these values has lost its credibility. Post-Calvinist entrepreneurs continued to scurry around busily accumulating capital long after serious belief in Calvin's God was no longer acceptable. Indeed, many of the unquestioned values of the West today are secularized forms of Judaeo-Christian values. Similarly also our ways of perceiving the future tend to be secularized forms of the three eschatological components of the Western religious tradition. The apocalyptic, the theological, and the prophetic perspectives on the future each has its corresponding modern secular expression; and each has its characteristic political style. My contention is that neither the apocalyptic nor the teleological perspectives in their contemporary forms provides an adequate perspective for a politics of the future. Only a recovery of the prophetic perspective will supply the ethos required for the political ethic required today. Each perspective must be understood both in relation to its history and to its modern secularized expression before a reasonable choice among them can be made.

1. *The apocalyptic perspective.* "Apocalypse" comes from the Greek word for uncovering, and normally refers to religious literature foretelling the imminent cataclysmic collapse of the present world order and the coming of a new era. Apocalyptic literature seethes with vivid symbolism, some of it obscure and esoteric. It is also characterized by a sharp dualism and lush mytho-

logical imagery. It is wrong to separate apocalyptic from prophetic literature too sharply. There are apocalyptic passages in the prophets that cannot simply be ascribed to later writers. Still there are important differences between the prophetic and apocalyptic literature. Apocalyptic imagery stems mainly from Iranian religious influences with their complex angelology, weird demonology, and a stark dualism that pits light and darkness, this world age against the next. Where this influence predominates the material was usually excluded from the Jewish canon and is now classed as pseudepigrapha (false writings). The most apocalyptic book to remain in the canon is Daniel. But this dualism is pointedly expressed in, for example, this verse from a pseudepigraphal book: "The Most High has made not one world but two" (II Esdras 7:50).

The reason the prophetic spirit usually excludes apocalyptic motifs is that apocalypse creates a mood of world negation, fatalism, retreat from earthly chores, and sometimes even a virulent antiworldliness. The apocalyptic vision often designates an elect company who will be saved out of the catastrophic ruination of the world in the approaching holocaust and can therefore become the ideology of various types of elitism.

There are several differences between ancient and modern apocalyptic moods. The most important is that while the ancients foresaw some kind of miraculous delivery after the cataclysm, their secularized modern successors see only the cataclysm itself. In fact they often seem entranced by the vision of cataclysm. This vision frequently inspires masterful literature and poetry. One thinks of Ezra Pound and W. B. Yeats. But when politics become apocalyptic, the result is often disastrous. Reason and morality flee before incantation.

Apocalypticism and politics are inherently incompatible. Politics requires a goal, a capacity to measure and evaluate the means available to achieve it, and a certain confidence that history will provide a reasonably stable arena in which to seek the goal. Apocalypticism denies all these. No earthly goals are worth holding since all are equally corrupt or illusory. One cannot think rationally about means since life is determined by irrational powers and malevolent forces. Rational action is useless because powers outside history and beyond human control will quickly bring the whole thing to a blazing end.

One can see the modern reincarnation of this apocalyptic mood in such a film as *Dr. Strangelove*. Although many liberals saw this film as an eloquent exposure of our lackadaisical acceptance of the nuclear stalemate, I agree with Susan Sontag that it was a deeply antipolitical exercise in chic nihilism, the modern nonbeliever's equivalent of apocalypticism. Miss Sontag says:

> For *Doctor Strangelove* is not, in fact, a political film at all. It uses the OK targets of left-liberals (the defense establishment, Texas, chewing gum, mechanization, Ameriman vulgarity) and treats them from an entirely post-political, *Mad* Magazine point of view. *Doctor Strangelove* is really a very cheerful film. Certainly, its fullbloodedness contrasts favorably with what is (in retrospect) the effeteness of Chaplin's film. The end of *Doctor Strangelove*, with its matter-of-fact image of apocalypse and flip soundtrack ("We'll Meet Again"), reassures in a curious way, for nihilism is *our* contemporary form of moral uplift. As *The Great Dictator* was Popular Front optimism for the masses, so *Doctor Strangelove* is nihilism for the masses, a philistine nihilism. (From *Against* Interpretation [New York: Farrar, Straus and Giroux, 1966], p. 149.)

Apocalypticism is at work wherever people simply decide to opt out of the political process and seek personal salvation or wait for the deluge. They may continue to be interested in politics, but only to inveigh against its total corruption, artificiality, and uselessness.

2. *The teleological perspective.* Those who reject apocalypticism today as an appropriate attitude toward the future often do so in the name of some form of *teleology*. The irrationalism of the apocalyptic is fought with the immanental reason of the

Greeks. For many modern secular people some sort of teleological view of man and the cosmos has become a substitute for traditional religious belief.

Teleology comes from the Greek words for end or purpose (*telos*) and for meaning (*logos*). It is that view of any series which explains it in terms of an end or goal. Aristotle said all nature reflects the purposes of an immanent final cause. Christian theologians took over this Aristotelian view and not only identified the prime mover with God, but made the "teleological argument" one of the standard proofs for the existence of God.

Modern secularized teleology takes a number of forms. It can fasten on history and see man's climb from the cave to the penthouse as a process whose total momentum exceeds the sum of the parts. It can be based in biology, like some of Loren Eiseley's books, and point to a Great Intelligence moving toward still unthought-of forms of life. It can be even more encompassing as was Pierre Lecomte du Noüy's *Human Destiny* (1947). The work of Teilhard de Chardin is also in part teleological. Despite the many disclaimers entered against him by paleontologists, he convinces many people by his effort to locate the human phenomenon within a purposeful cosmic process. But Chardin's thought transcends ordinary teleological approaches by suggesting that man holds the key to the next stage of the cosmic process and that what happens now is really up to man. Chardin's teleology ripens into prophecy.

It is easy to see an element of *hubris* in teleology. Man experiences himself as a purposeful creature. Unable to believe that the vast cosmos around him is devoid of such purpose, he projects onto it his own purposive style, and sometimes assigns himself a crucial place in the *telos* of the cosmos. Even secularized men often have a sense that there must be some purposeful intelligence somewhere, that the appearance of a whole universe of such enormous complexity could hardly have happened by mere chance. This gnawing mixture of hubris and wishful thinking, still persists even in people who have left conventional religion behind.

Teleology, however, like apocalypticism, fails to provide the perspective on the future needed for politics today. True, one can derive a certain comfort from the conviction that reality is moving toward a predetermined telos. But when this attitude informs our planning it can inhibit imagination and discourage radical new initiatives. Teleology obscures the fact that history is radically open, has no predetermined end, and will go only where man takes it and nowhere else.

The weakness of teleological thinking is that it puts undue emphasis on the "arche," the beginning. The telos is really the highest development of the arche. The whole oak tree is there in the acorn and has but to develop and grow. Teleology projects onto history, which should be the realm of radical freedom and responsibility, a way of thinking derived from nature, which is the realm of development and necessity. If nihilistic antipolitics is modern, secularized apocalypticism, then teleology is the nature religion of modern secular man. It has all the advantages of nature religion: it makes man feel a little more at home in the bewildering cosmos, a little closer to the plants, stars, and animals. But it has the same disadvantages. It obscures man's special character as a historical creature, as an animal with memory and hope who knows that if he destroys his world he can no longer blame it on forces beyond his control.

The most exciting chapter in the history of religion is the titanic struggle that went on between Hebrew prophetism and the nature religion of the Canaanites. It was a battle between two views of man. Was man totally enmeshed in nature, an expression to its vitalities and powers, or was man a historical creature, called by a God who acted in historical events and who required him to take responsibility for himself and his world on the way to an open future? Prophetism won this battle. It did so not by falsely extricating man from nature, or by subsuming the historical within the natural. It won, in effect, by bringing nature into history. The old Canaanite fertility festivals became occasions to celebrate Yahweh's promises for the future. In the cycle of planting and harvest there was no genuine future, but in the promises of Yahweh there was. For this reason the victory of prophetism over Canaanite baalism, though it took place long ago, remains important today. It assures the survival of a perspective on the future without which both planning and politics would seem futile.

3. *Prophecy*. Recent biblical scholarship rejects the notion that the advent of Israelite prophecy marked a radical new departure in Hebrew religion. Israelite faith had always been "promissory," that is based on a promise about the future rather than "epiphanic," based on the revelation of an eternal condition. Jürgen Moltmann says, ". . . the making present of the future in the threat of judgment and the promise of wholeness is not a special characteristic of classical prophecy but, quite to the contrary, classical prophecy is a special case of Israelite promissory faith" (*Theology of Hope*, p. 125).

For many reasons prophecy has often been mistakenly confused with soothsaying or divination. Nothing could be further from the truth. The Hebrew prophets, it is true, often used the contemporary rhetorical devices of their time, including envisioning the future, in their prophetic utterances. But their purpose was entirely different as was their view of history. The only reason they talked about the future was to get people to change their present behavior. They did so because they believed the future was not predetermined but could be changed. As Hastings' *Dictionary of the Bible* rightly says, "The first task of prophecy is to break the people's faith in the ritual stereotype of destiny" (p. 808). The Jewish scriptures make a careful distinction between the *roeh* (seers) and the *nabi* (prophets). A true seer, such as Tiresias in Sophocles' *Oedipus Rex*, can foretell only because the gods have already determined every man's future. The seer speaks not to elicit repentance and a new course of action, as the prophets did, but to warn someone that striving to evade his fate is futile.

The prophets talk about the future in terms of what Yahweh will do *unless his people change their ways*. Yahweh is free to change his mind. The future is *not* predetermined. All that is sure is that Yahweh, who has promised to persevere with his people, will not abandon them. We should not allow either the literary form of prophecy or its misuses by Christian fundamentalism as spurious proofs of the Christian message to divert us from its main impact: seeing history as the field of man's moral responsibility for the future.

Is there a moral ethos today that expresses prophetism as we saw for apocalyptic and teleology? I think there is. In contrast to apocalyptic, the prophetic mood has confidence in the worth of moral and political action. It visualizes the future of this world not as an inferno that ushers in some other world but as the only future we have and the one which man is unavoidably summoned to shape in accord with his hopes and memories. The prophetic mentality rejects the apocalyptic notion that this or that elect group can escape cosmic ruination or is destined to rule the rest of us. It sees all peoples inextricably intertwined in the future of the world.

Against the teleological view, the prophetic sees the *eschata* (the future) transforming the *arche* (the past) rather than vice-versa. It sees the future with its manifold possibilities undoing the determinative grip of the past, of the beginning. In contrast to most forms of teleology, prophecy defines man as principally historical rather than as natural. Without denying his kinship to the beasts, it insists that his freedom to hope and remember, his capacity to take responsibility for the future, is not an accident but defines his very nature. But most importantly prophecy sees everything in the light of its possibilities for human use and celebration. Without rejecting the influence of historical continuities, it insists that our interest in history, if it is not merely antiquarian, arises from our orientation toward the future. We write and rewrite the past, we bring it to remembrance, because we have a mission in the future. The Israelite prophets called the past to memory not to divinize it but to remind people that the God of the covenant still expected things from them in the future.

At its worst, Christian eschatology blurs and dilutes the Jew-

ish view of the future by allowing too large a place for apocalyptic ideas and by compromising with teleology. The prophetic
spirit, as we have shown before, can *utilize* both apocalyptic
and teleological imagery so long as it is not swamped by them.
It can use them so long as the basic fact of man's answerability
for the future is not obscured. Christianity has not always succeeded in maintaining this prophetic dimension. At its best,
however, Christian theology makes unequivocally universal a
hope for the future from which non-Jews had sometimes felt
excluded. The writer of the Epistle to the Ephesians reminds
those early Christians that before Jesus came they had been
". . . aliens to the commonwealth of Israel, strangers from the
covenants of promise, with no hope and no God in the world"
(Eph. 2:12). What Jesus does is not to countermand the
Israelite view of the future but to invite everyone to share it.

What would be the contours of a politics whose perspective is
determined by a prophetic rather than by an apocalyptic or a
teleological orientation toward the future? The answer to this
question cannot be given abstractly. Prophecy insists that the
future will be shaped not by invisible malevolent forces or by
irresistible inherent tendencies but by what men decide to do.
But this insistence on the radical openness of the future is never
proclaimed in general. It is implied in a prophetic demand for
moral action in view of this or that concrete political issue. Thus
a politics informed by prophecy, in this contemporary sense
of the word, will not be supplied with specific directives but with
what can be more accurately designated a moral perspective.

If apocalypticism can lead to nihilism, and teleology to a
certain cosmic complacency, prophecy produces both the terror
and the joy inherent in the recognition that the future will be
what man will make of it. No individual man holds his own
destiny entirely in his hands, but man's corporate future is now
up to us. This raises the stakes of politics. It makes both heaven
and hell a possibility again. As Leslie Dewart says:

All history is free and possible. . . . This means that

history can actually fail. A *real* and *eternal* (more precisely, definite, irreversible) hell is a real possibility, even if it is not a punishment willed by the Greek *dike* of God. For there is no divine decree that assures the inevitability (any more than there is one to forbid the actuality) of unending progress or the ultimate success of man. Even the definitive and utter failure of history as a whole is a real possibility, which is due to man's real role in it—though the unwavering Christian *hope* is that this real possibility will not in fact, with God's help, come to pass.

But prophecy also arises from the more basic assumption that though man can shape the future, he can never himself bring history to a close and thus preclude the risk of heaven and hell. The vigorous future orientations of many nineteenth-century thinkers were spoiled by their mistaken belief that after one more surge, history would be finished and man would triumph once and for all. Comte thought the coming of the positive age would do this; Marx saw in the classless society an end to the motion generated by class conflict. Even the nineteenth-century scientific historians thought at times that man would finally be freed from history by studying it. Each was guilty in its own way of a type of false messianism. For prophecy, as the Jews have almost succeeded in teaching the rest of us, the Messiah is always the one who *will* come. Man is not God. Since he cannot abolish his own freedom, he cannot terminate history. Therefore all his politics must be informed by a bold provisionality. The prophetic perspective frees us from having to build for eternity or solve things once and for all. There is no "final solution" for anything.

But this unconditioned openness to the future also allows prophecy to escape from the paralysis of past decisions and policies. The prophetic call always requires repentance, the candid recognition that one has made mistakes but will now do something different. Policies need not be papered over with spurious claims that they are simply extensions of decisions made in the past. Man is not only capable of innovation, the prophetic perspective requires incessant innovation and the continuous reappraisal of past policies because tomorrow will not be just an unfolding of yesterday's tendencies. It will include aspects of unprecedented novelty.

Chicken Licken thought the sky was falling, and in his panic to spread the news about it, he led a host of his animal friends into the sly fox's lunch pail. What had struck the apocalyptic fowl was not the sky; it was an acorn. But an acorn is no help either. No matter what we do with it, an acorn can only develop into an oak tree and nothing else. Can we set aside both falling firmament and sprouting spores as our images of history and act on the conviction that there is no future except the one we make? The answer to this question will be given not in our creedal recitations but in how we make our individual and political decisions in the years ahead.

# V

⊠

## The Church in
## East Germany

⊠

Near Alexanderplatz, the new downtown area of East Berlin, stands the hulking ruin of the old Protestant Cathedral of Berlin. Today, two decades after the war, it remains a pile of shattered wreckage and pocked stone.

Alongside the cathedral stretches Marx-Engels Platz, the scene of the massive May Day demonstrations, and across the square stands the new Council of State building of the German Democratic Republic. In a crypt beneath the cathedral floor lie the remains of illustrious clergy and nobility from the era of the Kaisers. Occasionally a small group of people gathers for a worship service in a temporary chapel in the crypt.

All around them, in East Germany and in the whole of Eastern Europe, a new world is being constructed in which God and religion have no public status. The question of what the church should do in a "postreligious era" is not a matter of seminary bull sessions for the Christians of East Germany; it is a hard fact of life with which they must grapple every day.

The Protestant church in East Germany, viewed in its his-

c

torical and institutional forms, is fulfilling precisely the prediction made by a German intellectual named Karl Marx one hundred years ago. It is dying out. Sunday congregations have shrunk. Fewer and fewer people bother with baptism. Religious instruction in the schools is no longer permitted.

But when one emerges from the cold crypt of the broken cathedral and looks for signs of church life in other places, the picture is very different. In no other country in the world is there such a variety of new forms of Christian existence. A kind of "postreligious church" is emerging in the German Democratic Republic today—a vigorous, young and astonishing virile kind of Christianity in a land where the post-Constantinian era has already arrived.

## New Shapes of Christian Existence

After a year in Germany—living in West Berlin but traveling almost daily through check point Charley to the fascinating city of East Berlin—I became convinced not only that the church in East Germany will survive but that it is engaged in advanced research for the whole of Protestantism as we now move into a world that, as Bonhoeffer said, has "already become a world without religion."

The Church in East Germany today provides a living example of possible new shapes of Christian existence in an increasingly secularized environment. Leaving behind the cocoon of Christendom, it is emerging into the new age of secular, technological society with a verve and *joie de vivre* that never ceases to astonish crepe-hangers from the "Christian West." It is producing a generation of young laymen who know what it is to make a conscious choice to live by faith in a country where it is no longer the "thing to do." Styles of worship and congregational life are being developed that befit a period when the ancient privileges of throne and altar lie buried in the crypt along with their departed custodians.

Equally important is the group of young theologians that is

being produced. Beginning with the heritage of Barth, they seek to discern the presence of God in a society that allows him no special place, and they believe, like Bonhoeffer, that just because they and their fellow citizens are so far from God, they may be closer than ever. The theological contribution these theologians can make to the ecumenical conversation is an invaluable one, and we will hear more from them in the future. They combine the traditional precision and *Gründlichkeit* of German theology with a refreshing this-worldliness lacking in most theological cerebration today.

What are the main questions they are facing?

(1) Radical secularization. The main challenge confronting the Church in East Germany today is not communism but the galloping secularization and rationalization of what was once a very traditional society. In this respect the situation is not unlike that in Western Europe and the U.S.A. It is simply more visible. Politicians in Communist countries do not feel called upon to invoke the deity in their speeches, and there are no prayers at the opening of the Party Congress or the meetings of the Central Committee. The public façade has been removed and secularization is seen for what it is, the social process that inevitably accompanies the development of industrial society.

Few East German theologians bother to bewail the march of secularization. The only ones who do are those who still hanker for the eventual return to that nineteenth-century amalgam called Kulturprotestantismus. For most, however, secularization is not something to regret but rather to understand, and to understand theologically. Many view it quite favorably as the occasion that calls the church to an exodus out of the stifling Egypt of Christendom toward a land that is promised but not yet revealed.

Drawing on the theology of Friedrich Gogarten and the sociology of Dietrich von Oppen of West Germany and Hans Hoekendijk of Holland, they believe that secularization has its roots in the Bible itself. The Old Testament God abolishes sacred realms and de-demonizes nature. Jesus Christ defeats the cosmic powers and turns the world over to man to shape and care for responsibly. Secularization is seen as man's coming of age, taking into his own hands the reins of responsibility, being made free from cultural coercions so that he can stand between God and his fellow man without mythological barriers getting in the way.

The need for a theology of secularization is pressing today. How is God present for contemporary man in a world where the inherited theologies of natural law and the orders of creation are being swept away? But a theology of secularization can be written only in a secularized society, and in this respect, the East German Christians may be in a better position than their Western brothers to formulate a theological response to the dechristianized world.

## "ALL MEN ARE BASICALLY GODLESS"

(2) Atheism. Again this is not a matter of theorizing. It is the question of how one lives with and communicates with people who are atheists.

In this setting blanket generalizations about atheism are impossible. In East Germany there are political atheists and scientific atheists and practical atheists. These are human beings with whom one works and lives, with whom Christians teach in the same school and do research in the same lab. Daily life with atheists makes necessary a theological understanding that goes further than the old Eisenhowerian formula that everyone should believe as firmly as possible in whatever god he chooses.

No, common life with atheists demands of Christians an open confession that all men are basically godless, Christians included, and that it is precisely those "without God" whom God has reconciled in Jesus Christ. The fact that the gospel has nothing to say to any of us unless we are in some sense without God places Christians and atheists together in a solidarity that makes wholesale indictments sound false and hypocritical.

Then there is the question of the relationship between the

methodological atheism, or at least the agnosticism, that informs modern science and Christian faith. In East Germany, as in many places in the West, it is necessary to separate off the presupposition of God, not only from natural science but from all *Wissenschaft* (technical learning), including of course whatever kind of social science is possible. Just as most natural scientists have already disposed of the need for presupposing a deity in their attempt to undertand the natural order, so social scientists in the East believe one can come to terms with human personality and social structure without including this factor.

This opens the way for conversations with Marxist social scientists, and there are some Christians who believe there is no necessary contradiction between Christian faith and most elements of the Marxist method of social analysis. "Whether I accept the principles of Marxist social analysis or not," said one young East German to me, "has nothing more to do with the gospel than whether I accept the particle or the wave theory of light." When I suggested that his theology might be leaning precariously toward a kind of Christological atheism, he countered with the opinion that this was probably more biblical than the non-Christological theism that seems to be the temptation of Western cultural religion.

In any case there is much more work to be done by all theologians on the real meaning of atheism. When one recalls the ancient rabbinic saying that the next best thing to belief in Yahweh is at least not to believe in idols, then atheism might in fact be much closer to biblical faith than the vague cultural theism of nominal Christians in the West.

As in other areas the issue between Christians and atheists in East Germany seems cleaner and more forthright. Nominal theists are disappearing. They are disappearing in the West, too, but not as quickly. Whatever else its value may be, the death-of-God movement may help lift the fog of cultural piety from the West. It may reveal us for what we are, people who really do not believe in God at all. Then the painful process through which East German Christians are now passing may come to our aid, reminding us in a new way that it is precisely the godless ones for whom the gospel of Jesus Christ makes any sense.

## RESPONSIBLE ACTION IN COMMUNIST SOCIETY

(3) Communism: not as a theoretical ideology but as the basic program by which the social, political, and economic life is organized. Here the question is how does a Christian do his share to help his society to become what the World Council of Churches (WCC) has called a "responsible society"? What does this mean for Christians who wish to participate in political life? Are the only real Christians in East Germany those who are digging tunnels under the Wall (sometimes with shovels furnished by American television companies)? How can Christians who seek to play a role in political life avoid opportunism and me-too-ism?

This syndrome of problems comes to focus in the question put by a young Methodist layman who reads everything he can get his hands on about political ethics, especially from the WCC's Departments on the Laity, and Church and Society. "Everything I read," he said "urges me to get in there and work in the political arena, to grapple with ambiguities, to get my hands dirty. Now let me ask just one question, does that mean *me*, here, or is that just for Christians who live in Western liberal democracies?"

Western Christians have rarely faced this question very seriously. We have not usually been willing to allow Christians in the East to cope with political responsibility within their structures as we urge politicians to do on this side. While we revel in the ambiguities of power and the need for provisional solutions and half-loaves that are better than none, we frequently demand of Christians in the East a purity and consistency that would be dismissed with a smile in the West as well-intended utopianism.

Thus we indict a Hromadka for not "speaking out" on the Hungarian uprising as if this were the final test of his personal authenticity, and we condemn other Eastern churchmen because they do not issue resolutions on things we know they must be against. We seem to want everyone to be a Western liberal regardless of the actual political situation in which he is living. We often deny to others the same right to situational response or prudential judgments that we so carefully defend for ourselves.

But despite the reluctance of Western Christians to support and encourage their work, many East German Christians are active in the power structures of their society—in factory councils, collective farm committees, city councils, and even in the national People's Assembly. There can be no doubt that some of these people are opportunists. But there can also be no doubt that many of them are dedicated Christians who want to share in shaping their society.

It is useless and even wicked to suggest to these people that their main task is to oppose communism or to weaken the regime. Further it is cruel and untrue to imply, as we often do, that they are at best misled, at worst disloyal, followers of Christ. Much more to the point would be our effort to help such people to work out the ethical and theological guidelines they need to live and make decisions in a society where parliamentary democracy and an independent judiciary are not part of the governmental furniture. In short, our ideas on the ethics of political decision-making are considerably more provincial and socially determined than we often think. Conversations with those Christians who are trying to make faithful political decisions in the Eastern bloc might help deliver us from some of our situationally induced shortsightedness.

## To Create a Mystery

In their confrontation with communism the Protestants of East Germany have a special responsibility. They live in the only Communist country where the vast majority of Christians are Protestants. Although one enthusiastic Protestant theologian may have overstated his case when he once said that "only in East Germany do the Communists have the opportunity to hear the real Gospel," it is certainly true that the confrontation here will be a different one from that which takes place in countries with an Orthodox or Roman Catholic tradition. There are of course many Christians in East Germany who simply refuse to take part in this conversation. But those who do have frequently noticed a remarkable readiness on the part of Marxists to go to the brink of revisionism in their efforts to understand what Christian theologians are saying.

One party member in East Germany told me at great length about some of the Protestant theologians he had been reading. Then he said he agreed with Marx that the church would die out, but he rather thought it would probably last for another two thousand years or so. Here the border between quantitative orthodoxy and qualitative revisionism is reduced to almost nil.

But the important thing to notice is that East German Communists, ordinarily among the most stalwart defenders of doctrinal purity, have not been driven to these theoretical adjustments by theological arguments. They have been forced to rethink their theories by the fact that Christians in East Germany have simply not fitted into the predictions of scientific socialism. They have not functioned merely as ideological defenders of reaction and counterrevolution as they were supposed to. They have not all fled to the West. They have not died out.

In a sense those Christians in East Germany who are not content merely to pray in the crypt validate a striking statement of the late Cardinal Suhard of Paris. This spiritual father of the French Worker-Priest Movement once said that it is not the task of Christians to advocate a program or ideology. Rather their task is to create a mystery, a mystery that cannot be explained by any human system of thinking and can finally only be understood as the grace of God.

The conversation between Christians and Marxists in East Germany and in other countries of the Eastern bloc is in its first stages. At the universities of Leipzig and East Berlin, young Marxist philosophers are writing doctoral dissertations on Helmut

Thielicke and Gogarten. A Marxist philosopher in Prague recently published a critique of dialectical theology. The same man gave an address at the European conference of the World Student Christian Federation in Austria (where he told the students he felt like one small lion in a huge cage full of Daniels).

When an East German bishop announced a public lecture on Christianity and Marxism, four hundred people crowded in to hear him; and when a conference for theological students on the same topic was held at the East Berlin Evangelical Academy in Weisensee last winter, it was oversubscribed.

Many East German Christians know that Marxism is not a passing phase. They realize most of them will be living with it indefinitely. They also realize that to refuse any proffered conversation is to refuse to believe that a Communist can modify his ideas or perhaps even be converted. And to disbelieve in conversion is to disbelieve in God.

## HOPE FOR THIS WORLD

But what does the East German confrontation with a godless society mean for us?

As this conversation unfolds, it becomes increasingly clear to many that while the weakest link in Marxism is its naïve doctrine of man, the thin spot in contemporary Christian thought is its lack of a viable eschatology, an understanding of God's intention for the world. The Marxist philosopher Ernst Bloch, who once taught at Columbia University, has made the assertion that the "principle of hope" that was the genius of early Christianity, a principle by which all reality was understood, is no longer to be found in Christianity; it has been taken over in our time by the Communists. It is the Communists today who look with confidence to the future, while Christians think wistfully of their lost provinces and departed privileges. Anyone who has talked with Marxists knows that there is an important element of truth in what Bloch says. What, then, should our response be?

It has become evident to me that Christians must regain a

hope for the *world*. Somewhere between existentialist theology and *Heilsgeschichte* we have lost sight of the fact that it is *this world* that God is redeeming, and this world cannot mean either my own decision-making center, somehow lifted miraculously out of the cultural milieu in which I am enmeshed, or a Beulah-land world that is in some curious way totally "beyond history." Without relapsing into easily realized eschatologies, or schematic philosophies of history, Christians must once again insist that our hope is not for the church or for individual souls, but for the world. And this hope must be given specific content.

The first thing East German Christians have had to do in recent years is to relinquish false hopes. They have had to learn not to live year after year in the enervating expectation that deliverance was coming from the West. They have had to learn that it is on Christ and not on young Lochinvar that their hopes should be centered. And Jesus Christ "comes on clouds from heaven." Whatever that may mean it is clear that he does *not* come riding a tank through the Brandenburg Gate.

I think we in the West have cheated and misled our fellow Christians in East Germany by our constant suggestions that rescue is on the way. We do it every time an American politician, including John F. Kennedy, makes a speech at the Wall. It it time to be honest with ourselves and with them. If the East Germans were not "liberated" on June 17, 1953, when they fought tanks with paving blocks, or on August 13, 1961, when a wall was erected through the middle of what is still ostensibly a "four-power" city, is it fair to continue to suggest to them that if they just hold out a little bit longer, rescue will come? I do not think it is.

It is a terrible thing to die in the waiting room, and I believe we should tell our fellow Christians in the German Democratic Republic that, despite all our reservations about the questionable legality of their regime and the human tragedy of their separation, they should serve God with a whole heart where they are. As a young layman told me recently, "I cannot look my East German neighbor squarely in the eye, whether he is a

Communist or something else, if I am constantly glancing over my shoulder toward the West."

He was right. I have not said much here about the political situation as such or about the Ulbricht regime with which, needless to say, I have very little sympathy. But I do believe something important is happening in East Germany today. In an era in which deities and divinities will soon be no longer accorded even summary deference, it is something from which we can learn and for which we can be thankful.

# VI

❈

# New Phase in
# Christian-Marxist Encounter

❈

THE DIALOGUE BETWEEN CHRISTIANS AND MARXISTS NOW GOING on in both Eastern and Western Europe has entered a new phase. It has now begun to flow into the larger theological stream, bringing with it new currents that are sure to influence the theological tides.

The previous phase began when the late Pope John XXIII issued his epochal encyclical *Pacem in Terris*. One section contained a paragraph indicating that contemporary social and political movements should not be opposed merely because of the ideologies once connected to them. The Pope gave Christians explicit encouragement to work in cooperation with non-Christians in the struggle for peace and human dignity.

Nothing less than the whole "fortress" psychology implied by the church's previously unswerving opposition to communism was now thrown into question. From the millions of Catholics in East European countries already far along various roads to divergent types of "liberalization," one could almost hear the immense sigh of relief.

The change in Rome's attitude has enormously affected that of Protestants also. It was especially important in the arena of intellectual and philosophical conversation. What had been mostly a clandestine dialogue between Christians and Marxists came out in the open after 1963.

When I visited Prague in the summer of 1964 after a year's absence I was astounded at the change in the scope of the Christian-Marxist encounter. Both Christians and Communists seemed much more at ease and open to discussion. Young German and Czech Communists, whom I had once met furtively by night, now sat with us in sidewalk cafes. Even in East Berlin I talked for two hours in a restaurant with an SED (Communist Party) member with whom I had never been able to exchange a word in public in previous years.

All evidence indicates that during the past year the Eastern European dialogue has continued to broaden and deepen. The same holds, though in a less spectacular way, for the West. In some instances contact has been established at places where virtually nothing but epithets had been exchanged for twenty years. More importantly, the dialogue at some points begins to show signs of emerging from its "confrontational" to its "cooperative" stage, of moving from mutual self-explication to common discussion of cognate problems.

## ITALY: PROMISING CONFRONTATION

I will mention first some of the crucial contact points, especially in Western Europe, then go on to hazard some guesses about where the new stage of the dialogue may be heading.

Italy is the natural starting point, for there we find Western Europe's largest Communist Party. It is the home of the late Palmiro Togliatti, whose posthumously published testament, in which he urged Communists to discard their antiquated, antireligious bias, is one of the crucial documents of the encounter. It is also the place where the dialogue often appears most promising.

One example is a recent issue of the international socialist journal published in Rome, which is devoted almost entirely to the Catholic-Marxist dialogue. Another is a book entitled *Il Dialogo alla Prova* (Florence: Editions Valechi, 1965), which brings together essays by five Communists and five Catholics. No doubt the book is a trifle out of balance since the Communists speak for the recognized intellectual elite of the party while their partners represent that group of Catholic Left writers who appear in such progressive periodicals as *Testimonianze* and *Il Gallo*.

The man most responsible for the book is M. Gozzini, a Catholic who edited it with the Communist Lombardo Radice. Gozzini invokes the memory of John XXIII and calls attention to several recent pronouncements of the Italian hierarchy that use the term "atheistic communism," which he believes to be in contrast to the spirit of Pope John. Gozzini asks whether these two words must *always* appear together like salt and pepper, and suggests that one purpose of the dialogue is to see if they might be separated.

Gozzini emphasizes that the dialogue must begin with religious and theological issues and not with politics, although he concedes that the political implications must eventually be confronted.

The Communists who write in *Il Dialogo alla Prova*, on the other hand, unanimously urge the need for social and political cooperation on key issues before anything else. They enjoy, even relish, the dialectic of the discussions, but they do not believe it will develop sufficient consensus to allow for effective social action soon enough. They always want to discuss things that seem premature to Catholics, and their attitude evoked constant reminders from the Catholics that this was a conversation "between persons, not parties." No doubt this is an important distinction. It is one, however, that contemporary Catholics can make much more readily than Communists can.

In any case, their primarily political orientation did not prevent the Communists from talking philosophy and theology. Radice, for example, jettisons completely the old Communist slogan that religion is "the opiate of the people." It arose, he says, from a totally different historical milieu and is simply untrue today.

Other Communists point out similarities between the values of Christianity and communism. One of them, edging toward what I call the new phase of the dialogue, writes at some length about the philosophy of Teilhard de Chardin, declaring that his notion of man's responsibility for the development of the world lies very close to the perspective of Marxism.

So far the Italian dialogue has taken place largely between top Communists thinkers and a somewhat amorphous group called "the Catholic Left." It has not had much explicit encouragement from the Vatican and has not been popular among the lower echelons of Communist workers, some of whom may suspect that a "dialogue with Catholicism" may mean they will have to start talking with their wives.

A breakthrough to the grassroots may come, however, with an astonishing film, *The Gospel According to Matthew,* a life of Jesus directed by the Marxist Pier Paolo Pasolini. The firm has already received widespread Catholic recognition, and Pasolini hopes it will greatly broaden the dialogue. Like Radice, Pasolini rejects the idea that religion must always be the opiate of the people. He constantly exhorts fellow Communists to get into conversation with Catholics. His film has had even more impact than his speeches in achieving this objective.

## FRANCE AND GERMANY

In other Western European countries, things are proceeding much more slowly. The blanket of Gaullism in France has smothered some of the enthusiasm for dialogue that once blossomed there. Since the demise of the Worker-Priests, who had fashioned a real bridgehead of conversation, rank and file interest has been sporadic. In intellectual circles, however, the exchange flows on unabated.

American readers can savor some of its flavor in Lucien Gold-

mann's *The Hidden God* (New York: Humanities Press, 1964).
Originally a Romanian, Goldmann is a follower of the Hungarian
Marxist sage Georg Lukàcs. Although *Le Dieu Caché* was first
published in 1955, it remains a good clue and a useful introduc-
tion to the subtlety and sophistication of the French dialogue.

Goldmann sees important similarities between Christianity and
Marxism, both of which he identifies with the Augustinian heritage. Also, he knows a lot about the centrality of the utter
hiddenness of God in Christianity. He knows more in fact than
some of our happily morbid American theologians, for whom
God's absence can only mean his certain death. Deeply familiar
with the role of the *deus absconditus*, Goldmann provides a brac-
ing antidote to the wearisome linguistic excursions into talk about
"God-talk" that busy so many Anglo-Saxons today. As we shall
see in a moment, his discussion of transcendence as the pressure
exerted by the future on the present will become increasingly important as the next phase of the discussions unfold.

West Germany presents particular problems to a Christian-
Communist *détente*. First there is the division along lines that,
despite the efforts of many Christians to avert it, is often seen in
a "God vs. atheism" way. Also, any attempt at Christian-Marxist
dialogue in West Germany today labors under an obstacle we
previously faced in the United States: one party to the conversation is illegal.

Consequently, when Horst Symanowski, the pioneer of modern
German industrial mission, wanted to arrange a Communist-
Christian dialogue in Mainz-Kastel near Frankfurt in the winter
of 1964–65, he had to import the Communists from East Germany (though there were West Germans present who, if the SED
were legal in West Germany, might very well belong). To add
another dimension, Symanowski also invited some Christians from
East Germany, where some sort of dialogue is, willy nilly, a part of
every Christian's life.

The story of this historic confrontation is a fascinating one.
Listening and responding to their six guests from beyond the Wall
were one hundred and fifty West Germans. In astonishment they

heard Karl Ordnung, an East German Methodist lay preacher, tell an SED member where they differed. They heard an East German Marxist ask whether it is not heresy or unbelief to hold, as some Western Christians do, that Christian existence is impossible under an atheistic state. They heard the Communists, including Max Hauschke of the East German National Assembly, talk about errors their country had made in foreign policy. Pastor Bruno Schottstädt, director of the East Berlin Gossner Mission, talked about "solidarity between Christians and non-Christians" and pleaded with his fellow Christians not to see him as a "fifth column for the West."

The Gossner consultation was an important one. Even though little progress was made either politically or philosophically, the simple fact of having it was a major triumph. It may signal a new and growing willingness among Germans to begin to talk across the various barriers that divide them.

### EVOLUTION AND HOPE

Where will the dialogue go? Already there are signs that a new and significant phase has begun. Some participants are begining to probe the theological and political significance of the *fact that the dialogue exists*. Writing in *Trybuna Ludy*, the organ of the United Polish Workers (Communist) Party, the writer Boleslav Wojcicki points out that "dialogue" means more than just "conversation." It means a commitment to the partner, a willingness to listen, respond, and change. He insists further that, despite Catholic hesitancy, some degree of political cooperation is essential since the dialogue occurs only where the social environment supports it.

Marxists constantly emphasize that only by working together in the alembic of social conflict will Communists and Christians make any progress in theoretical palaver. *Praxis* precedes theory. But this is not just a Marxist point. It also coheres with one of the most important contributions of modern theology, that real theologizing must arise from the church's painful engage-

ment with the world. Theology does not consist in axioms refined in theory and then applied in practice. Theology is the
church thinking about its *praxis* in light of its history. When
the participants begin to ask what the fact of dialogue means for
the character of existence and the way thinking proceeds, the new
phase has begun. Confrontation is over. Cooperative intellectual
labor on a common problem has begun.

But the church, and the Communists as well, also thinks in
light of the future, and this points to the key theological issue
in the new phase. It could be stated in the form of a simple
question, "What may man hope for?" Both Christian and Marxist
thinking should be defined by *praxis* in light of hope. Put more
technically, the issue is the relationship of history to eschatology.
Here theology reveals its intellectual pocket of poverty. It needs
help. Traditional Christian eschatologies have usually been so
inward or so transcendental that any hope *for this world* has
been erased. Or if not this, they have uncritically identified specific
utopian visions with the Kingdom of God.

But neither of these routes will suffice any longer. There are
widespread indications that this dialogue in Europe may soon
merge with the enormous renewal of interest in eschatology, as
evidenced for example by Jürgen Moltmann's widely discussed
new book *Theologie der Hoffnung* (München: Christian Kaiser
Verlag, 1964; ET *Theology of Hope*, London: SCM Press, 1967).

Moltmann emphasizes that eschatology is not simply one
among many in the catalogue of Christian doctrines. Rather it
determines the ethos of all Christian thinking. This new interest
in eschatology, prefiguring a serious exchange with Marxism,
was symbolized at the annual theological colloquium at the
Evangelical Academy in Tutzing. The subject, selected because it
seemed to be the most pressing of theological issues, was "Evolution and Hope." The two figures discussed were the maverick
Catholic Teilhard de Chardin and the renegade Marxist Ernst
Bloch. Thus does the "dialogue" begin to find its way into the
larger movement of Continental theology. It has only started to
have an impact on the main issues of theology and has hardly

even begun to influence the most significant discussions among Marxists.

It would be wrong to suggest that in either Teilhard or Bloch, or in some admixture of these two fascinating thinkers, a new theology of the future will emerge. True, both saw vividly what the Germans called the *"Impuls der Erwartung,"* Teilhard in natural evolution and Bloch in history. Both saw the enormous significance for man of his new power to apply science in fashioning his own destiny. Both were highly suspect by the purer ideologists of their respective camps, but this is to be expected since any worthwhile theology of the future will certainly need to break with established positions.

Still there is a missing dimension in both men. Teilhard saw in the logic of evolution a deepening humanization of man. Bloch was concerned with "Man-as-Promise" and what he called "the ontology of the not yet." But both failed to deal with the questions of how and why history or evolution nurtures the continuing humanization of man. Neither dealt satisfactorily with the theme of sacrifice or, in Christian terms, with the Cross at the unavoidable doorway to the future. Neither Teilhard the Catholic nor Bloch the Marxist grappled seriously with the somewhat Protestant notion that even hope itself is not a natural endowment of man but a gift from God.

Still both men belong to the indispensable avant-garde of theology without which the necessarily pedestrian work the rest of us do would become insufferably boring. Their points of similarity indicate that as theology emerges at last from its paranoid existentialist phase, as it grows restless with the word games of linguistic analysis, certain forms of revisionist Marxism and some strains in natural science may provide new and much more stimulating discussion partners for the theologian.

Providentially, this happens just as the dialogue between Christians and Marxists ceases to be a hobby for deviants on both sides and begins to press the very questions that all must deal with. Thus phase two of the dialogue may combine with the newest threshold in theology.

The prospect is a fascinating one, and as Jürgen Moltmann shrewdly suggests, the old basic ground rule of theology, *credo ut intelligam*, may give way in an age of reborn eschatological thinking to *spero ut intelligam*. Hope rather than belief may become the category through which we think as men of faith. When that happens, a serious dialogue with the Marxists, those who have spelled out in one way or another the hope that motivates half the people on the globe, will no longer be an option. It will become a necessity.

# VII

❖

# Kafka East, Kafka West

---

❖

THE COSMOPOLITAN CITIZENS OF PRAGUE LIKE TO THINK OF THEIR exquisite city as the *"Treffpunkt Europas,"* a meeting place for dialogue in the heart of Europe. For many years now this has hardly been the case. Crouched under the largest statue of Stalin anywhere in the world, the "Golden City on the Moldau" seemed grim and gray. Tourists avoided it, or couldn't get in. Creative intellectual life slowed to a standstill. But by the summer of 1964, Prague had begun to look once again like its old self. The enormous statue of Stalin had been painfully dismantled and discarded; the lagging Czech economy had experienced a slight upturn; and most importantly, Prague had begun once again to entertain world conferences, delegations, and floods of Western tourists.

One such conference was the Second Assembly of the Christian Peace Conference which in June brought over twelve hundred churchmen from nearly one hundred countries to Prague for a week of discussion and study on the Christian contribution to world peace. Arranged in part by the Protestant host churches in

Czechoslovakia, the conference caused many Eastern European officials to hold their breath apprehensively. It was the biggest assembly of churchmen ever brought together on Communist soil. The Czech Christians were thrilled that Prague seemed to be playing its old role as broker of ideas. Once again Americans, Italians, and even Germans were sitting in Prague's picturesque bistros and cellars, inundating its museums and shopping along the Vaclavske Namesti. Some were attending the showings of the Prague International Film Festival which opened with a new Czech film extolling the courage of those sturdy few who had stood up against repression during the Stalinist midnight. Others took in performances of the plays of Swiss playwright Friedrich Dürrenmatt, who had come to Prague personally to open the series, knowing full well that as recently as two years ago his plays (*The Visit, The Physicist*) had been banned by the Communists as confused bourgeois jottings. At the galleries in the Stáre Mesto, bold, abstract paintings attracted crowds of enthusiastic viewers. In short, Prague had begun to look and feel very much like Warsaw must have felt in 1956 and 1957.

Both Eastern and Western Europeans were reveling in the new freedom, and no one was enjoying it more than the Czechs themselves. Together everyone enjoyed the freshets of the new Czech thaw, an era of cultural openness for which the writer, Franz Kafka, a Czech Jew who wrote in German, has become a kind of inclusive symbol. In fact Kafka now serves almost as the posthumously rehabilitated and now canonized patron saint of the kind of cosmopolitan *élan* Prague would like so much to recover.

But for the Christians of Europe, Kafka represents something even more. The strident controversy which has emerged among Communist regimes about his rehabilitation, after he had languished for forty years in the limbo of "bourgeois decadence," dramatizes the strains and fissures which are emerging among the various Eastern European countries. It is not quite a "realignment," but patterns of relationships are shifting, and this is taking place in a Europe which thinks of itself less and less as "East" and

"West" but more and more simply as "Europe." The loosening which has developed out of relaxation of both the Russian and of the American grip over their respective spheres of influence in Europe has naturally produced a tendency on the part of the European nations to look toward each other again.

The shrine of the new Kafka cult is a small but skillfully contrived exhibit in Prague's Museum of Czech literature. There visitors from many foreign countries mix with Czech citizens to view with hushed reverence the autographs, photos, and manuscript pages. The exhibit was opened by none other than old Max Brod himself, the crusty dean of the Kafka scholars, making his first visit to Prague since he fled before the occupying Germans in 1938. The exhibit is an event of epochal cultural and political significance in the life of Eastern Europe. In the forty years since Kafka died, his works had not been available in Communist countries. Now that period of exile is over. In this unostentatious exhibit, the Czechs were in effect announcing to the world that culturally they are once again joining Europe.

But culture and politics can never be separated for very long, especially in Central Europe. The fact that the Czechs had decided to join Europe culturally had far-reaching political implications. The strain it has put on intra-Communist relations is illustrated by the now-famous consultation on Kafka which was held at the venerable old Liblicá Castle near Prague in May of 1963. The host was Professor Edvard Goldstücker, Czechoslovakia's leading expert on Kafka. The discussion included writers and critics from most of the Eastern European countries as well as two Western Communist literary lights, Ernst Fischer from Austria and Roger Garaudy from France. Monsieur Garaudy is not only a respected philosophy professor but is a member of the politiburo of the French Communist party. The upshot of the consultation was the total defeat of the die-hard East German delegation headed by Alfred Kurella, whose word has been definitive in East Germany on matters of culture politics. The Western participants were calling for the open publication of all of Kafka's works, most of the

Easterners agreed. Some of the Polish and Czech writers even saw in Kafka a kind of socialist before his time. Others insisted that he was the supreme commentator on the alienation of modern man in industrial society and that, furthermore, this alienation obtains not only in capitalist but also in socialist societies. This latter bit of Marxist heterodoxy, which shocked and antagonized the East Germans, was urged especially by Fischer and Garaudy.

Reports have it that Herr Kurella and his delegation of cultural Stalinists became increasingly apprehensive at the direction the consultation was taking. They had come to bury Kafka not to praise him. As the hours lengthened and tempers shortened, the walls of Liblicá Castle rang with charge and countercharge. Finally, as one Marxist liberalizer sang yet another paean to Kafka, describing him as a kind of "morning dove heralding the new day of socialism," Herr Kurella could stand it no longer. "A dove?" he shouted. "This Kafka is no dove of the morning. He is a bat flying out of the darkness." With that the East German delegation returned home. To this day it is impossible to buy a copy of Kafka's works anywhere in East Germany.

A central reality in the emergence of the new "Europe" is that East Germany, the last remaining bastion of cultural repression and literary Stalinism, is becoming more and more isolated in every way. Travel between Poland and Western Europe today, for example is much easier than between East Germany and Poland. The East Germans resent the effort of the Czechs to increase trade and tourism with West Germany. As the Czechs move swiftly toward an open door to Western Europe, the provincialism of the isolated East Germans becomes even more evident in contrast. East German intellectuals are increasingly testy and confused about the new turn of events. "Sure the Czechs can do it," grumbled one young East German Communist to me, half in resentment, half in jealousy, "but that's because they don't have any 'West Prague' to worry about."

His sour-grapes attitude illustrates the dreary plight of East Germany. It lives daily in direct contact with a country which uses the same language and draws on the same cultural tradition, but with which it continues to be locked in a continuing political and propaganda imbroglio. Neither East nor West Germany can resist the temptation to criticize and belittle the other, to turn every conversation into a brawl. The Poles and the Czechs do not have any such problem. Still, it remains a question how much the East German regime uses the galling presence of the West German *"Revanchismus"* as an excuse to avoid a cultural liberalization it has no stomach for anyway. In any case, the intellectuals of Eastern Europe, Communist and non-Communist alike, are contemptuous of the East Germans.

All of this lies beneath discussions about the place of Kafka or other disputes over so-called culture politics. It means for the churches of Europe that, whether they live in the East or the West, a solution to what is called "the German problem" stands high on the agenda of prerequisites to a lasting peace. Czechs are understandably unnerved when high Bonn officials suggest that the Sudeten question is still not finally settled. They are also disturbed by the new haughtiness emanating from Pankow. Most European churchmen, East and West, are apprehensive about Germany and feel that a real danger to the peace exists so long as the U.S.A. and the U.S.S.R. continue to use their respective halves of Germany to advance their own aims in Europe. Many now long for a "European" solution, letting the Germans work out their own reunification within the framework of a European security arrangement. The feeling remains that until something is done about Germany, a constant danger to the peace of Europe continues to smolder.

This concern on the part of Europeans comes as a surprise not only to Americans, whose major interest in Germany is the recent modest success of neo-Nazi parties, but to Africans and Asians, to whom the whole dispute seems only to deflect attention from the real issues that churches should be facing. European Christians, however, seared by the memories of war, feel very strongly that the preservation of peace is the *sine qua non* of human life on their little continent and for this reason is the most important aspect of their social witness. This may be why *Pacem in Terris* received a much wider and more sympathetic reading among European Protestants than it did among their American counterparts. It may also explain why the constant irritation produced by the unsolved division of Germany, together with the appearance of a whole new set of relationships among European nations, seems so much more important than it does on this side of the Atlantic. The Kafka controversy reflects the tensions and troubles, as well as the healthy possibilities, of the new "Europe" that is now replacing the two Europes which have existed side by side since the dropping of the iron curtain.

But there is a more properly theological reason why the Kafka issue is so significant for the life of the churches in Europe. Kafka represents that point at which a conversation between Christians and Marxists now seems to be possible. His writings do this by posing with unavoidable clarity what one writer has aptly called "the atheist's problem of God."

A German-speaking Jew, reared in the Prague ghetto, Franz Kafka wrote with such power because he fully accepted the radically immanentist world of twentieth-century man, a world in which the three-decker universe of classical religious metaphysics had disappeared. But in accepting this de-religionized world, he also revealed its limitations, even its contradictions. His novels and short stories demonstrate that man cannot be truly man in such a world. At the same time, they show that man cannot go back to the irretrievably vanished world of classical Christendom. Like the Italian writer Ignazio Silone, Kafka wanted to find real grace, but to find it in this world. His anguish in failing to do so puts an unavoidable question to Christian and Marxist alike, a question which, despite the Marxist revisionism of Leszek Kolakowski and Milan Mahovec, and despite the Christian "revisionism" of Paul Tillich and Dietrich Bonhoeffer, has still not been answered. But there is no doubt that it is *the* characteristic religious question of modern man.

As W. H. Auden once said, if we think of the relationship

Shakespeare bore to his age and Goethe bore to his, then Kafka
bears that kind of relationship to ours. It is Kafka, the troubled,
half-believing Jew, who may bring Christians and Marxists back
into useful and lively conversation. How can Kafka do this?

Kafka's work elicits a major concession from both Christians
and Marxists. From those Christians who take him seriously he
demands that the traditional God of the world overhead be forgotten as no longer anything more than a cultural accessory to
man. The theologian who tries to bring grace to twentieth-century
man by dragging him back to a vanished metaphysical worldview
is defeated before he begins. This is especially true of Europe. To
touch the European man of today, the grace of God must be
understood in terms which do not violate the radically terrestrial
horizon within which he lives. Kafka paints the figure of a man in
quest of meaning, bewildered and beset but sure of one thing: the
meaning he needs is not available at the wellsprings of traditionally defined religion. To Christian theologians, Kafka's challenge
is one that they can ignore only at the risk of becoming intellectual antiquarians.

But to Marxists, Kafka's question is equally disturbing. He
testifies to the prolonged spiritual anguish of a man who, while
recognizing the one-dimensionality of existence, still insists that it
is impossible to live within it. While rejecting salvation from the
God of traditional theism, Kafka also refused to bow down before
the easy explanations of scientific atheism. He realized, decades
before the many young Marxist theoreticians who have now
learned it, that man's alienation from himself and his neighbor
points to a dimension of his existence which far transcends his
participation in the economic and political institutions of human
society.

Kafka learned this in the hardest way possible: through trying
to overcome his feeling of estrangement in life by burying himself in the vitalities of human community. He wanted to be a
good man, a good husband, a good father. As fate would have it,
he was denied most of the supports of communal life, but not
before he had learned that they provide no sure bulwark against

the assaults of alienation. Beginning with a naïve faith that solidarity in the human community would deliver him from his lost-
ness, Kafka slowly had to admit to himself that in fact the whole
human community was lost. There was something basically and
elementally wrong at the very core of existence, something that no
revolution, no matter how comprehensive, could remedy.

It is the residue of alienation, still persistently present in socialist societies, which puzzles honest Marxist thinkers today. Their
puzzlement is increased when they meet Christians, especially
those who have grown up in socialist societies and unashamedly
call themselves socialists, but who insist there is a restlessness in
man even under socialism, a quest for meaning to which only the
Christian Gospel can speak. Kafka is no propagandist for the
Gospel. But he does make it impossible for sensitive young Marxists, who cannot avoid finding their own deepest feelings probed
and articulated in his pages, to defend the rickety proposition that
human estrangement disappears when private property is abolished.

This explains in part why such Marxist scholars as Milan Ma-
hovecs, who is professor of ethics at Prague's Charles University,
are now devoting so much time to the study of Christian theologians, why they seek out visiting churchmen for extended conversations. It also explains why those timorous theologians who,
frightened by the Marxist onslaught, retreated into a two-king-
doms theology to avoid dialogue or, even worse, tried to accommodate Christian theology to dialectical materialism, now find
themselves in a painfully embarrassing position. The young Marxists who roam the cafes of Prague in search of dialogue are not
interested in some sort of theological me-too-ism. They are look-
ing for Christians who will take them seriously, as thinkers and as
human beings, who will criticize their position relentlessly, ex-
plicate their own point of view clearly, and listen to the Marxist
position with neither arrogance nor ingratiation.

After many years of ideological cold war, what Jean-Paul Sartre
has called the "disarmament of culture" may be getting started.

Christians have at last taken up the long delayed but desperately needed conversation with the Marxists. Perhaps now, as the Catholic-Protestant intra-familial conversation we have presumptuously called a "dialogue" produces a growing ecumenical consensus, the *real* dialogue with the world can begin.

In Kafka's haunting novel *The Trial*, he depicts Joseph K. gazing at a picture on the cathedral wall of Christ being lowered into the tomb, with a knight in attendance. Here Kafka has recalled to us the blackest moment in man's long story, that moment when the link between God and man seemed irreparably broken. It was in this darkened world of the absent God that Kafka groped during his whole career. But because he suffered the pain of the absent God in his own life, and wished desperately for something more, he may provide the starting point for a conversation between those who, reared in belief, find it hard to believe, and those who, reared in disbelief, find it even harder to disbelieve. Somewhere in the midst of this candid dialogue, the God who stands beyond belief and disbelief may be glimpsed again.

# VIII

⊠

## Let's End the
## Communist-Christian Vendetta

⊠

> In my opinion, the world will not be converted to the
> heavenly promises of Christianity unless Christianity has
> previously been converted . . . to the promises of earth.
> —*Pierre Teilhard de Chardin.*

It is certainly time to bring to a close the decades-long war of
attrition between Christianity and communism. Nothing more ex-
acerbates the global confrontation between East and West than
the rhetoric that bills it as a duel to the death between God and
atheism. Nothing so adds lethal danger to the Vietnam war as the
twisted misconstruction of it into an Armageddon between the
knights of Christian civilization and the dragons of godlessness.
Propagandists of the church and of the various communist parties
have stoked the fires of frenzy without ceasing. One reason why
Americans find it so difficult to think rationally about world
revolution is that they have been fed so long on the strident anti-
communism of the American churches. Who could count the
communion-breakfast speeches, sermons, and pastoral admoni-
tions that have drummed up the image of a world struggle be-

tween the hosts of God and the hosts of Satan? Or—a more subtle form of the same propaganda—the number of times we have been asked to support Christian missions, rally behind foreign aid, contribute to Radio Free Europe, even defend land reform, because if we did not those whom we denied our concern would certainly become Reds?

Either religion in one of its forms or Marxism in one of its varieties is now the controlling life view for most of the world's people. At the same time thermonuclear weapons have made the Thermopylae interpretation of this state of affairs infinitely dangerous. Is there any possibility that in the last third of our war-weary twentieth century the two protagonists in this deadly, dagger-drawn duel can begin to work out a way of living together?

Two books appeared in the fall of 1966 that suggest we may be on the threshold of a new era in communist-Christian relationships. Since 1964 a group of (mainly Catholic) German-speaking Christians called the Paulus Society has been meeting with a group of European Marxist intellectuals. One of the most articulate of these Marxists is the Frenchman Roger Garaudy. Out of his experience in the developing conversation Garaudy has written a short book tracing the changed attitude of Catholics and communists alike to the fact that they inhabit the same planet. The American Catholic publishing firm of Herder and Herder had the book translated from the original French and issued it under the title *From Anathema to Dialogue*. This was an unprecedented move, since Herder had never before published a book by a communist. Therefore the firm asked Leslie Dewart, a Catholic who is professor of philosophy at St. Michael's College of the University of Toronto, to write an answer to Garaudy. Professor Dewart agreed, producing a book entitled *The Future of Belief*, a kind of companion volume to Garaudy. These two volumes, both of them milestones in American religious thought—Garaudy's because it exposes Americans to an intelligent and sympathetic Marxist critique of religion rather than to the inane testimony of cosmonauts who reported that they had not seen any angels; Dewart's because it takes the Marxist critique with the utter seriousness it deserves and then moves on to the first stages of a risky but enormously imaginative reconstruction of the doctrine of God.

## I

Together they provide more than enough thrust to lift theological discussion to a new level of interest and clarity.

Like any Marxist, Mr. Garaudy believes that the emerging dialogue is possible only because of today's changed social and political conditions. Among these are the one-third of the world which is now in some way communist, the rapid expansion of science and technology, and the throwing off of colonial rule in Africa and Asia. (He might have cited two other events sometimes classified by insurance companies as "acts of God," namely the death of Stalin and of Pope Pius XII.) But Garaudy also emphasizes intellectual currents. He mentions the favorable theological atmosphere induced by Barth's movement from *The Epistle to the Romans* to *The Humanity of God*, by the efforts of Bultmann and his followers to distinguish between the real gospel and dated, prescientific world views, and by the impact of Bishop John Robinson's *Honest to God*. All this, he says, has led both Christians and Marxists to a new appreciation of "what is basic" and what is not in their respective points of view.

It is not surprising that in his chapter on the Christian rediscovery of what is basic Garaudy makes large use of Teilhard de Chardin. He praises Teilhard not only for his attempts to save Christianity from its doltish opposition to science but for his insistence that no man can be saved "except through an extension of the universe," as the Jesuit paleontologist once said. Garaudy also agrees with Teilhard's dissent from the usual interpretation of the doctrine of original sin—an interpretation Teilhard called "the tight collar which strangles our minds and hearts." Garaudy is not the only Marxist with a soft spot for this Roman priest. He is admired especially among the young unorthodox European Marxist intellectuals.

Garaudy puts considerable stress on the contrast now being

made between the "Constantinian tradition" in Christianity (close connection with the ruling classes, assimilation of Greco-Latin ideologies and their hierarchical conception of the world) and the "apocalyptical tradition" of primitive Christianity. The latter, as Garaudy sees it, reflects the period when Christianity was "a slave religion, . . . a protest, however weak, against the established order, and a hope for the coming of the Kingdom on earth as in heaven." In fact Garaudy, following (perhaps unconsciously) an old tradition in left-wing Christianity, has a theory of the "fall" of the church. Luther held that the fall of the church occurred in the fifth century, with the development of centralized papal authority. Garaudy pushes the fall further back, as did Münzer and Hus, into the fourth century, when Christianity became "an ideology of imperial justification and resignation."

But in Garaudy's opinion the fall did not finish off Christianity. This Marxist seems delighted at what he takes to be the rebirth in our time of that apocalyptic tradition. He cites with enthusiasm the Jesuit Karl Rahner's characterization of Christianity (at the May 1965 Salzburg Christian-Marxist colloquy) as "the religion of the absolute future." And Garaudy obviously relishes today's rebirth of interest in the eschatological aspect of theology. In this connection he mentions the brilliant young Roman Catholic theologian Johannes Metz. He might also have mentioned such Protestants as Jürgen Moltmann and Gerhard Sauter.

II

It is clear that a dialogue between Christianity and Marxism is now possible. Both are talking about the full development of man (humanization and hominization). Both are concerned, each in its own way, with subjectivity and transcendence. Both are fascinated with the future and what it means for man's freedom, maturation, and responsibility. But, as Garaudy realizes, the question now becomes: Is a dialogue *desirable?*

From the Marxist side, he says, the answer is an unequivocal Yes. Marxists seek to incorporate into their thinking all that is

D

humanly valuable, wherever and however it has arisen. Garaudy is especially attentive to the epochal contribution Christianity made to civilization when it defined man as a free agent in time. He finds it hard to hide his enthusiasm for this part of the Christian theological tradition. He says:

> With Christianity, a new status for man in regard to the world appeared, one which constituted a radical departure from that of Greek humanism. Existence, for man, is no longer a matter of being inserted into the Whole of the cosmos as one of its fragments. For man to exist has now become the liberation from his nature and his past, by the divine grace revealed in Christ, liberation for a life which consists in free decisions. As of this moment, authentic "history" has become possible: to the timeless contemplation of the eternal laws of the cosmos, there succeeds an unfolding of life in time, where the past is the *locus* of sin, where the future which lies always before us is the *locus* of grace, and where the present is the time for decision, the time for acceptance or rejection of the divine call.

I quote this section at length because it sums up better than many Christian theologians could the unique thrust of biblical faith: setting man as a responsible agent in history before an open future. Far from being a sacralization of the present or a canonization of the past, Christianity requires us to understand everything in the world in terms of the future, on the basis of what it could become if its potential were fully unlocked.

So dialogue is both possible and desirable for Marxists, at least for Garaudy. Unfortunately Garaudy cannot speak for Marshal Lin Piao and the Chinese Red Guards, or even for the East European communist establishment. That many East European communists were denied visas for the Salzburg meeting indicates that in the minds of party hierarchs there remain considerable reservations about dialogue with Christians. Garaudy does not specifically mention this aspect of the problem, but he does concede that some Christians may find the frequent administrative harassment and occasional persecution of Christians and churches in communist countries an obstacle to honest encounter. These abuses he attributes to the narrow, rigid Marxist view of religion still held by many communists—a view he himself has often criticized openly. He is especially hard on communists who say they are ready to talk with Catholic workers, but "as workers, not as Catholics."

Yet this will not quite do. Possibly the horror stories in the right-wing Catholic and Protestant press about the persecution of Christians "behind the iron curtain" are somewhat exaggerated. Nonetheless it is true that, especially in the U.S.S.R., pressuring the seminaries and legal pestering and closing of churches seem far from abating. One could of course point out that in Indonesia's recent anticommunist coup four hundred thousand persons suspected of being communists or having communist leanings were murdered. If that many Christians had been killed, by communists or anyone else anywhere in the world, we should never hear the end of it. As it was, there were but a few ripples of protest. Now everything seems to be forgotten, and we are rejoicing that Indonesia has "turned back from communism."

Still, countering accusations with accusations will never work. Garaudy is right in saying that Christians must decide whether they really want dialogue with communists, that no one else can make this decision for them. If they want dialogue they will have to accept certain preconditions. The first—which must be rigorously observed by both sides—is that one does not seek to destroy the dialogue partner. Garaudy holds that Marxism has now reached a stage where it not only can but must converse with Christianity. He knows that the problem of the person, of what he calls "subjectivity," is central for the next phase of Marxist theoretical development. He believes that in rejecting all of Christianity, Marxists have been insufficiently dialectical since Christianity is "right in the questions it raises about man and history" and wrong only in the answer it gives. Marxism, however, has not even begun to raise these questions. It must raise them now, and so dialogue is needed.

## III

In no sense a rebutal of Garaudy's, Professor Dewart's book is an attempt to respond to the Marxist critique of religion and of other elements that engage modern sensibility by undertaking a further constructive development of Christian theism. Thus it is a book about God and the doctrine of God—happily so, for not only does this approach meet the Marxist challenge precisely where it must be met, but it brings a powerful new contribution to bear in a theological situation still reeling from the recent "death of God" foray. It is perhaps unfortunate that Dewart has subtitled his book "Theism in a World Come of Age." True, he is trying to purify and sharpen for modern minds the concept of what it means to believe in God. But his solution goes so far beyond any previous types of theism that this subtitle may mislead. In his *The Courage to Be* (the 1954 Terry lectures), Paul Tillich talked about a God "beyond theism." But in comparison with Dewart's Tillich's ideas seem cautious. It is Dewart's God rather than Tillich's who is "beyond theism."

In Dewart's very first chapter, "Christian Theism and Contemporary Experience," the reader becomes aware that he is in for a new departure in theological writing. The author insists that the everyday experience of twentieth-century men can no longer be simply discounted by theology, or attributed to error or cultural backsliding. Christians and non-Christians alike, he says, we are all part of the contemporary experience; hence it will not do to define the issue as merely "communicating" some sort of Christian idea to those outside. The church communicates itself; its task is to integrate itself with the modern world, not to sell it a product. The real issue is the self-evident conflict between faith and the *prima facie* experience of today's secular world.

## IV

In attacking this problem Dewart makes grateful use of the critics who have uncovered the sources of the religious illusion, especially Freud and Marx. His citation of these two men is crucial not only because they present the most potent critique of religion but because both view religion in the context of personal or social development. Freud does not blame man for having religious illusions; he merely doubts that these illusions will endure now that science has come to the center of the stage. On his part, Marx refused to join the intellectual atheists of his day in trumpeting their version of death-of-God thinking. Except for a brief period early in his career, he had little interest in theism or atheism as such. He realized that religious systems spring from particular types of socioeconomic structure and that theism would disappear when the social conditions that fostered it had been abolished, not in the face of verbal tirades. "The philosophers have interpreted the world in various ways," he said in his *Theses on Feuerbach,* "but the thing to do now is to change it."

Dewart likewise concedes that a certain form of theism might have been necessary and, given its historical setting, even healthy. But just as infants grow up and discard their childish fantasies, so societies require, and develop, conscious changes in their symbolizations. Dewart does not fault the church for the various doctrines of God it has elaborated in order to live in different historical periods. But he does insist that the development must now go further, that "Christian belief in its traditional form is at its most basic level not attuned to the contemporary experience of man. . . ."

What can be done? Dewart proposes a doctrine of God which moves completely beyond the classical epistemologies and metaphysics out of which our Christian concept of deity grew. He refuses to become enmeshed in a dispute about whether God "exists," since he considers mistaken the very notion of "existence" or even of "being" as prerequisite to reality. To exalt being as the ultimate category of reality not only traps us in static categories of thought but inevitably produces a political ethic which cannot make room for radical change. Thus Dewart—obviously a master of scholastic thought—also shows that he has understood the main point of the Marxist critique. He knows that doctrines of God reflect the social structure of given historical periods, but that after they have been elaborated they can retard social change by sacralizing the structures of the period in which they emerged. This circumstance explains why some type of atheism is always necessary for social change. It also explains why the atheist who takes himself too seriously reveals his own mental enmeshment in the same outdated period. Thus neither theism nor atheism can be "absolute." When either becomes absolute it denies the irreducibly historical character of any religious or antireligious belief. Both theism and atheism need to be aware of their conditional character and of their need to develop and change if they are to escape the rigidity of dogmatism.

Marxist atheism, unlike "death of God" atheism, is conditional, not absolute. It does not object to the doctrine of God abstractly or to any and every doctrine of God in general. It expressly denies the Christian doctrine of God as this doctrine has emerged and developed in history. And it objects to this doctrine not because of some esoteric vision of God's demise or because the notion seems empty to many people, but *because of what the Christian belief in God has done to inhibit man's maturation and to thwart social change.* Responding to Marxist atheism is thus a totally different thing from responding to "death of God" atheism. There is no conceivable doctrine or idea of God that could satisfy those who seriously believe in the "death" of God. Death is final. This is what makes their position ahistorical and incapable of development. For Marxist atheism, on the other hand, a doctrine of God that met their specific objections would at least move the conversation further along. Dewart does us all a momentous service by showing that it is atheism of the Marxist type, not of the death-of-God type, which is the real challenge to theology today.

Because it is conditional atheism that must be answered by a further development of theism, Dewart insists on our leaving firmly behind the unconditional theism of historical Christianity. We must energetically "dehellenize" Christian theology. This step calls for jettisoning the entire metaphysical framework in which our idea of God is housed. Here, Dewart in fact believes, Marxists have not gone far enough, have not been critical enough of their roots in Hegel and in idealism. Marxism "is not radical enough," he declares. "It is not enough to overcome idealism. It is also necessary to overcome metaphysics as a speculative ideology."

## V

Dewart's final chapter, "The Development of Christian Theism," sketches an idea of God that does "overcome metaphysics as a speculative ideology." The author "overcomes metaphysics" by allowing himself to imagine how the doctrine of God might develop if it were reconstructed to meet the needs of our actual experience, not of metaphysical coherence. Such reconstruction could, for example, leave behind the "pre-occupation with God's existence which characterized post-patristic thought, and hence post-medieval philosophy," and go on to work out what the fact of our *experience* of transcendence means. Dewart believes that in the process we could stop worrying about whether God exists or is a being, because we do not have to identify intelligibility with being. In other words, it is not necessary that something exist in order to have reality; it is only our Hellenic bias that makes us think so. The future, for example, does not "exist" and has no "being" in any sense; nevertheless it is a reality in human experience.

What about God's "personality"? Dewart holds that this idiom must also be left behind in the next stage of Christian theism. The modern idea of personality restricts the reality of God and makes some form of atheism necessary. In a brief but enticing passage Dewart speculates on a view of God that could go beyond personal metaphors: "The typical experience of the disaffiliated religious person today is that 'God could not possibly be a person. He must be some kind of cosmic force.'" A naïve view, Dewart concedes. But he also thinks that it may express a correct hunch that God, rather than a center of being, is "an expansive force which impels persons to go out and beyond themselves." He even suggests that this naïve notion represents a legitimate indictment of one aspect of absolute theism, and that even so crude an insight "may yet be redeemed in the future of Christian theism."

No doubt this author's contribution to our understanding of God will anger and bewilder many Christians. It makes use of the Catholic assertion that doctrine "develops"—a venerable principle that served both Cardinal Newman and Karl Adam, though those gentlemen hardly foresaw what Dewart would do with it. Dewart employs the category of development not to justify what happened between a doctrine's beginnings and its present form, but to show what *could* happen to the present form, to make it viable in the future. How for example might the traditional idea of God's "omnipotence" be transcended? By letting "omnipotence" mean what it must, Dewart says; namely, that the world is totally open to God and therefore "totally open to *future creation by man*." . . . "The case," he adds, "is not that God can do the impossible . . . but that for God all things are possible—and that therefore with God all things are possible to man." Thus the static idea of God's omnipotence would be transformed into a belief in "the radical openness of history—an openness which not even man's freedom can annihilate." The ethical consequence of this belief is twofold: we could no longer fall back on the superstitious notion of divine omnipotence, and we would have to take adult responsibility for the world. We would know, Dewart says, that unless we make it, "the Kingdom of God [will] never come."

This transformation of the idea of God's omnipotence demonstrates what startling possibilities open up if we recognize the need to develop further our present doctrines. It also joins the issue with the Marxists, in superb fashion. The Marxists' main objection to Christian theism is that it inhibits man from assuming complete control of the future. Engels, for example, says in his *Anti-Dühring* that "men themselves make history, only they do so in a given environment which conditions it, and on the basis of actual relations already existing." This famous sentence reveals one of Marxism's unresolved quandaries. Does man *really* make history and is the future *unconditionally* open? Or is there in history some "inner logic" to which man must ultimately conform if he is to be "free"? Marxism remains unclear on this point. At times Karl Marx's thinking seems to be influenced by a Hebrew view of the future as something utterly subject to man's free moral action; at other times his links with the Stoics and more particularly with Hegel conspire to reduce man's freedom to a kind of acquiescence in the inevitable dialectic.

## VI

A viable Christian doctrine of God today must make man *more* responsible for history than Marxism does. In fact this, to my mind, is a decisive test of the adequacy of the doctrine for our time. Christianity—to quote Rahner again—"is the religion of the absolute future." Therefore it must break its ties with any belief in a fixed plan being worked out in history; and must recast its idioms of transcendence in such a way that transcendence is seen as that unconditionally open future which elicits man's unreserved freedom in shaping his own future. Obviously the test of such a doctrine's validity could not be theoretical; it would have to be operational. Whether—or that—God is real is decided not by argumentation but by action in history, by politics.

This new frame of reference for theology begins to shape up in Dewart's book. History itself now provides the inclusive horizon for theological thought. Thus Dewart rejects those notions of the incarnation which think of God as coming into terrestrial history on a sort of slumming jaunt. God, he insists, has taken up permanent residence in history, indeed becomes the very substance of history. The last supratemporal and extraterrestrial metaphysic is rinsed away and we find a God who is totally "with us" in the human enterprise. Thus Dewart represents a thorough-going incarnationalism, rather than the quasi-docetic incarnationalism that has plagued theology for so long. God is that presence within history which is not a part of history but makes history possible. This concept links Dewart to the recent school of eschatological theologians in Europe—such people as Gerhard Sauter, Johannes Metz, Jürgen Moltmann. These theologians also see God as the pressure for maturity and responsibility exerted on man by an unequivocally open future. If the word "God" has become too freighted with metaphysical overtones, Dewart is ready to accept a new word to designate this reality. "Wise people," he says, "do not worry about names."

*The Future of Belief* is not easy reading. By a process of careful and qualified reasoning it arrives at astonishing conclusions. Dewart does not simply toss out his spectacular assertions; he constructs them with meticulous respect for clarity of argument. But his cautious style of writing makes his ideas even more breathtaking. He avoids side issues and plunges into the very heart of the matter, the question on which our faith lives or dies; the reality of the living God. In my opinion, we either move along the road Dewart has staked out or else we abandon any pretense that we can find a viable doctrine of God for our time. Dewart is right in saying that, failing such a doctrine, atheism is the most attractive alternative for the modern intelligence.

There is but one danger in this book: it is so persuasive that it may deceive us into thinking that Christianity's dispute with communism can be resolved by argument or even by "dialogue." It cannot. We learn from the Marxists what we should have known from the Bible: that truth is always found through experience, rarely through disputation. The question is whether Christianity or communism will contribute more to man's desperate need to "come of age," to his education for reality, to his capacity for accepting unequivocal responsibility for whither history now goes. Jesus said that if we know the truth it will make us free. We must now also recognize that whatever makes us free is *truth*.

[1] The two books discussed in this chapter are published in England as follows: Leslie Dewart, *The Future of Belief: Theism in a World Come of Age* (London: Burns & Oates, 1967); Roger Garaudy, *From Anathema to Dialogue* (London: Collins, 1967).

# PART THREE

## RECOGNIZING THE NEW ERA—
## THE CHURCH AND THE FUTURE

# IX

⊞

## The Signs of the New Era

⊞

In his remarkable book Young Man Luther, the psychologist Erik Erikson tells about the trip the young Luther made to Rome in 1510 at the age of twenty-seven. Luther's diary for that trip reveals that he completely missed noticing any sign of the Renaissance. He remarks about the elegant ancient aqueducts, about the church-operated hospitals and orphanages, but seems never to have been struck by the paintings, sculpture, or the spirit which to us today seem so clearly to have signaled the birth of a new historical period.

In 1510 Luther was a medieval man with a medieval world-view, even though the Renaissance was in full blossom around him. Erikson goes on to make this telling observation: "It takes time, especially for deeply preoccupied people, to comprehend the unity of the beginnings of an era which later will be so neatly classified in history books" (p. 175).

When we as churchmen ask "What is the mission of the church in our time?" we ask it as deeply preoccupied people. We are thus perhaps congenitally least able to appreciate the radical newness of the context in which we minister. We have a vaguely troubled awareness that something is going on around us whose scope and dimension we only dimly discern. We live as modern men at the dawn of the post-modern age. The "scene is changing" and, as when in the world of the theatre the scenes are changed, it means a new act is about to begin.

Our suspicion that we stand at the beginning of a new phase in human history finds support in the perceptive voices of our time. Romano Guardini and Paul Tillich say it is the "modern age" or the "Protestant era" which now draws to a finale. More seriously, Dietrich Bonhoeffer, the German pastor-martyr, writes of a world which has "come of age," has outgrown religion itself. Martin Heidegger insists it is not just the modern period, but the whole western epoch which began with the Greeks, that is now over.

A new age is symbolized by a "new man," a new identity image. Here the modern seers are confused. Who is this post-modern man? We cannot tell. We see him more now for what he is not than for what he is. As Hendrik Kraemer says, basing his description on Camus' *The Rebel*, he is post-individual, post-moral, post-religious. In short, he is a living embodiment of everything the religious, bourgeois individualistic man of the classical Protestant period is not.

What shall we say to the heralds of a new era? It can be one of three answers. We can say, as many of us do, that they are wrong, that the world in which we are living is essentially the same as the one into which we were born. We can persist as modern men in a post-modern age to the puzzlement of future generations, who will wonder how anyone could have misread the signs of the times so obtusely.

Or, if we choose, we can listen to the warnings and believe them, as most of us do, but continue to act as though nothing were different. This appears to be at once the most anomalous and the most popular alternative.

The third possibility is the most awesome, but in my view the only authentically responsible one. It sees the paradox underlying the way we ask "What is the church's mission in today's world?" It sees that this is a question asked by an institution whose vocabulary, organizational forms, and style of life grew up in one age, about how it relates itself to a world whose whole life style and self-understanding is increasingly informed by the new age.

If we choose to believe the new voices and to live as a church in the emerging post-western era, then we must ask the most basic question of all: How can the church now die to itself in the old body so that a resurrection to new life is possible? The question is a vexatious one. But we have some clues on which way to proceed.

The spectacular new interest in biblical studies and the growth of ecumenical theology have come just at the outset of a new chapter in the history both of the church and the world. We have been reminded especially of three rich truths about the church's commission which had lain idle over many years. First, the World Council's study commissions and documents have helped us recognize again that Christ is Lord not only of the church but of the world. In fact, he is present for his people *only in* the world. So we find God and serve him only as we do so *in* the world.

Second, the exciting emphasis on the ministry of the laity has forced us to recoil from a grave distortion of our view of the ministry. We now see in a fresh way that Jesus shares his ministry with his entire church, and that the ministry of the laity within the life of the world should be the central focus.

Third, we have been forced by the ecumenical conversation to strip away the cultural addenda and look once again at the essential nature of the church. In the hard light of its biblical calling, we see the church again as *laos theou*, as a servant people of a Servant God. We have been shaken to realize how far the church had strayed. We see again that its *sole* reason for existence is to make known God's love and peace. As burning is to fire, so is mission to church. It has no other nature.

The striking feature of this ecumenical renaissance is that these three insights, on the church and its ministry and on the presence of Christ in the world, correlate so naturally with what we can know about the new-emerging age. The remainder of this chapter will endeavor to demonstrate the character of this historical and theological reciprocity. It will attempt to show how the "answering theology" of the church meets the most salient features of the erupting new epoch.

### 1. The Post-Moral Man and the Church as Mission

The new man has been called "post-moral." Perhaps a more precise designation would be post-moralistic. The world no longer conceives of moral principles as absolutes, but as functions of a particular historical period, class outlook, or psychological stance. As citizens of this age we have seen some of our dearest "Christian principles" unmasked by Freud and Marx as merely "western," or "bourgeois," or even "Victorian." Reinhold Niebuhr has instructed a whole generation in the degree to which the strategies of our own personal and national self-aggrandizement are subtly baptized as altruistic virtues springing from God's holy will. A communist revolution and a rising of the colonial peoples have been necessary to convince us that the gospel, which seemed so universal to us, had within it components which to some people smacked of capitalism and imperialism. We can hardly blame these people for failing to distinguish between the essential gospel and its white-western caricature when we remember that this is a distinction most Americans still find difficulty in seeing.

We live in a world which can never again look an absolute moral principle in the face without asking for its ideological credentials. In this world of competing relativisms, what can the church do? Should it cling with increasing ferocity to its cherished "principles," many of them spawned in a robust period of frontier individualism, and decry the "moral collapse" around it? This has been the posture of the dying remnant of every *ancien régime* in history. Or should it realize that the Christian gospel is *not* the summons to a particular moral code at all—but a living enactment, the coming kingdom initiated by Jesus? The gospel is a word addressed to moral cynics and ethical absolutists alike, a word which finds all our ethical pretensions filthy rags and reconciles men to each other with no reference to their level of moral attainment.

The church which sees its task as mission does not stake its life on any particular ethical system. Rather it lives in the world, and speaks and sings, freed from the "bondage to the law." It is free to love as only those who have first been loved unconditionally are able to love.

Karl Barth says the church is the "provisional demonstration" of God's new humanity. It acts out in the world what God has done and is doing not just for the church but for the world. It is a people whose total life, in every responsibility and in every relationship, makes known this fact: that God is establishing a new humanity where social, racial, and ethical hostilities have been abolished. The church is that part of the world where God's hidden presence is made visible, tangible, audible, and evident.

We have been reminded through the course of contemporary history, as has happened so frequently in the past, that the church is *not* called to be the judge of the world. There is one judge, who judges both church and world. His people share deeply the tensions, the pain and the longings of the world, but are never defeated or captured by it. If through their life of concern for sinners God judges the sin, it is his judgment, not theirs. An age which has found its moralisms slanted and contradictory needs not a law but a gospel. It calls for a church willing to enter every concrete human crisis and struggle there for whatever reconciliation and justice can be wrung from the situation itself.

## 2. Christ in the World and the Post-Christian Era

The church's willingness to plunge into radical solidarity with estranged human life arises from its confidence in the second of the newly rediscovered truths of biblical faith: that Christ is present in the world helps us know how to live faithfully in a post-Christian era.

By "post-Christian" our modern seers mean that we now live at a time when the basic issues and most profound questions of human life and destiny are no longer framed in the language of the classical Christian tradition. No longer do a Dante and an Aquinas, one a poet, the other a theologian, share the same conceptual framework. Even the more recent paradoxical relationship of a Jonathan Edwards and a Herman Melville to the same awesome Calvinist world is now gone. Order has broken down while various worldviews compete for mastery. Christians now for the first time since the earliest centuries begin to live as a minority.

At this crucial juncture, as the *corpus Christianum* breaks up around us, as "western Christendom" melts into an international technical society, we are again affirming that it is in the *world* that Christ is at work, redeeming and renewing.

Again Dietrich Bonhoeffer has said it well. He wrote toward the end of his life that we must remember it is the *world* which has been altered by the Cross and Resurrection, not just our inner lives. Since the Incarnation, he insists, the believing man does not have to look back and forth in agonized hesitation between God and the world. He need not try to "apply the one to the other," as though the atonement had never occurred. For "since the event of Jesus Christ, we cannot look at the world without seeing God, or look at God without seeing the world." Christ is present for his church in the world. The movement toward him is a movement *toward* the world, not away from it. As the writer of Hebrews has put it: "Jesus suffered outside the gate in order to sanctify the people through His own blood. Therefore let us go forth to Him, outside the camp, bearing abuse for Him" (Heb. 13:12,13).

Markus Barth in an article in the *Scottish Journal of Theology* (Vol. XII, No. 1, pp. 32ff.) argues persuasively that Jesus' own baptism was not a separation or withdrawal from the world, but an entering into solidarity with those who have nothing to confess but sin. It was a rejection of the mediated religion of the temple and a public attestation of what God had done for all men in Christ. In our own baptism, Barth argues, we declare not our separation from sinners but our oneness with them and God's love for them and us.

Likewise in worship we affirm God's presence in the world. Though he discussed it in terms of the "real presence of Christ in the elements," Luther's polemics, as Vilmos Vajta indicates (in *Luther on Worship*, Muhlenberg, 1958), really grew out of his belief in the omnipresent God. "The Incarnation was the real offense." He insisted on Christ's real presence in worship against those Catholics who attributed it to a priestly miracle and the enthusiasts who located Christ in the heart of the believer. For Luther, Christ was *already* present, regardless of priestly liturgy or the level of our inner religiousness. Nor do the elements change into something else (as in transubstantiation), for Christ is present "in, with and under" the elements. And his presence at worship, made evident by the Word, opens our eyes to his presence in the world, where he had previously been hidden. This was Luther's argument.

Thus, Christ is present in the world for both believer and nonbeliever. He is there whether we have faith in him or not, and before any religious words are spoken. He is Emmanuel, "God with us." He does not change the world into something it is not by his presence. It is still politics, still education, still business. He is there—in, with, and under the essential forms of the world. The manner of Christ's presence in worship thus opens our eyes to the way he is present in the world. He is there because he has chosen to be there, not because our piety or ceremonial bring him there. He was in the world before we were and will be there when we are gone.

Both baptism and worship point to a Christ who is known only in the world. And "world" as it is used in biblical language is not a spatial term. As Ernst Troeltsch says, ". . . it is not a cosmological conception at all; it is a term composed of political, social, and economic elements." The New Testament uses "world" to refer not to the stage, but to the actors in the drama of history. The church must find its Lord in the secular world.

Protestant piety has reduced the dimensions of the Christian claim. We have taken the earliest Christian affirmation "Jesus Christ is Lord," a confession which expresses the exultant sweep and cosmic scope of God's intention, and substituted for it the pietistic diminutive "I accept Jesus as personal Saviour." Though the latter phrase is insisted on most tenaciously by those who claim to be closest to the Bible, the phrase itself never appears in the New Testament, and there is little scriptural justification for it. It reduces the cosmic claims of the gospel to the manageable dimensions of an inward individualism.

God is present in the world, whether or not we happen at this moment to feel his presence in our hearts. We do not carry him to the world somehow previously devoid of his presence. We meet him as he calls us to him in the world where he is already.

Thus God's presence in the human world does not cease because of a recession in the number or the piety of believers, or the passing of a style or religious language. God survives the post-Christian era because he does not need our theological formulations to conjure him into existence. The passing of the language of Zion merely means we must learn to speak to the world in its own terms. This means that we must listen, for God speaks to the church in the language of the world. Only when we have learned the world's language can we speak again of God. The world, its character, its hopes, its meaning, its destiny, becomes the *content* as well as the *context* of our speaking.

### 3. Post-Individual and the Ministry of the Laity

Taking the problems of the world seriously, loving it and learning its language—these all point to the third and perhaps most important of the recent theological insights, the ministry of the laity. The lost battle cry of the Reformation, "the priesthood of all believers," has been found again in a sharply focused way. We have begun to see the ministry of the laity, not as a "religious task" (it has nothing to do with ushers and acolytes), but as a ministry of reconciliation of service expressed in political, occupational, and intellectual terms in the secular world itself. This permits a nonindividualist view of conversion. A man's conversion to Christ does *not* involve his *removal* from the interaction nexus of secular society. (This is what George

MacLeod has condemned as "extricationist theology.") It is rather the transformation of his whole way of living within the relationships of society. It is not the conversion of an "individual," thought of as in abstract isolation from society. Rather it is the transformation of a "person," of one sector of the culture's complex relationships as they are consciously lived and uniquely styled in the experience of a particular human being. To become a man of faith is not to add one more responsibility to the ones we have already; it is to fulfill the ones we have in a new way.

Modern man grasps his identity through his personal style of life. But the identity he grasps is mediated to him by constant interaction with his society, his family, his work, his community. Thus the achievement of a personal identity is a *social* phenomenon. The "new life," or "new self," which is the gift of God in Christ, is likewise a social self. Conversion too is a social process. It is just as impossible to be a Christian merely inwardly as it is to be a father, employer, or citizen inwardly. All these are social-relational designations, hence Pascal's famous dictum, "an individual Christian is no Christian."

Thus the ministry of the laity is not a "religious ministry" in the ecclesiastical sense of the term. It is a relational, reconciling ministry expressed within the secular matrix of the world. It is the church's primary ministry in our age. The clergy's job is not primary but derivative. Its significance is drawn from its service to the primary ministers, the laymen. The clergy serve as "ministers to the ministers," as "kitchen troops in the divine army" (to use Hans-Reudi Weber's simile). And kitchen troops should be court-martialed if they confuse the fighting men, either by adjuring them to spend more and more time in the mess hall, or by implying repetitiously that the only truly military job in the army is that of kitchen officer, while the rest are not really "full-time."

The changing scene demands a new stratagem. Can the church change? Can it meet the post-modern man by living out through its laity the mission with which the God who lives in the world has commissioned it? The obstacles are formidable. The familiar ways of our fathers are comfortable and, if increasingly irrelevant, still secure. The new world is frightening and untried. But the call is unmistakable: "Get out from your own country and from your kindred and from your father's house, to a land that I will show you . . . and by you all the families of the earth will be blessed."

# X

⌘

# The Coming World City

⌘

FUTURE HISTORIANS WILL RECORD THE TWENTIETH CENTURY AS
that century in which the whole world became one immense
city. We know already that America is an urban civilization.
Not only is our society becoming a series of superurban regions—
the Boston to Norfolk megalopolis, the Great Lakes megalopolis,
the West Coast megalopolis—but even in the interstices, in up-
state New York and downstate Illinois, life is being urbanized.
The undulating tentacles of highways and the searching eye of
the TV screen draw even the remotest hamlets into the web of
urban thinking and living. In one lifetime America has changed
from an agricultural to a metropolitan nation.

But America is not the pacesetter in urbanization. Overseas
the transformation is even more jarring and accelerated. In fact,
the most portentous phenomenon of our time is the urbanization of the non-western world. The cities of India, for example,
are growing at the rate of 50 percent per decade. They will have
to absorb one hundred forty million new immigrants from the
villages before the end of this century. Carts circulate through

the teaming alleys of Calcutta every morning to shovel the dead from the sidewalks. The city is glutted by a daily increment of babies from heaven and immigrants from villages. But Calcutta's real problems lie in the future. Unless its growth rate is greatly retarded, its present population of two-and-a-half million will have swollen to the staggering figure of sixty-six million by the turn of the century. The story is the same everywhere. Latin America's urbanization is proceeding much faster than North America's, and the most urbanized society in the whole world today is probably not the United States but Japan. Tokyo has almost surpassed London as the world's largest city.

But what is the city really?

The city exists wherever the environment nature has provided is consciously transformed into the setting for human life. The city is that place where the stuff of the universe becomes the raw material for man's projects. In our epoch, the whole world is quickly becoming "city." Cities are the artifacts of man. But whereas they once formed mere islands in a vast sea of uncharted nature, today the balance is reversing itself. The world is becoming one huge interdependent city, in which jungles and deserts remain only with the explicit consent of a global metropolis. Yesterday's wilderness provides today's green-belt or park, and the mountains and seas, once barriers to man, have become his facilities for water sports and tourism.

It is thrilling to live in the age of the new world city, but as we look at it more closely its deep ambiguity is also evident. It displays all the terror and promise of New York or Los Angeles. It is a city of vivid contrasts. The psychotic splits we now feel within our own cities: between slum and suburb, between rich and poor, between white and colored also rend the new world city. The chasm between the inner city and the residential reserve on its borders has torn the world into a series of ghettos surrounded by luxurious estates. America and Europe, perhaps the whole northern hemisphere have become the white suburbs to which people have withdrawn to try to forget the furious revolts now raging through Latin America and Afro-Asia. The grotesque gap between satiated consumers and starving children is all too evident. Just as differences in status, income, and color have fractured the body and broken the spirit of the American city, these same lacerations threaten to push the new world city into a frenzy of self destruction. Just as suburbanites lock their car windows as they drive through the Negro districts of our American cities, or stare in fascinated terror at the riots which seeth through their streets, so we in the West, and this includes Americans and Russians, watch with growing apprehensiveness the similar rebellions which boil up in the Congo, in Vietnam, in the Dominican Republic. We have a hunch that the Harlem riots and the Vietcong raids are not entirely unrelated, and we are probably right in our hunch. As a Negro taxi driver remarked to a Negro social worker when the newspapers announced the Chinese had exploded a nuclear device, "I see by the paper that *we* have a bomb. Now maybe they won't shove us around so much!" America and Europe have become the Shaker Heights and Wellesley Hills of the world.

As we look more closely at the new world city we see that, like the cities of America, it is really *two* cities. It is the city of life and the city of death. It is the city of choice and the city of necessity. In response to an interview, an Egyptian youth said in 1962, "Why should I stay in my village? It's dreary, dark, and dirty. There's nothing to do in the village, no movies, no fun! Anyway the land could not support both me and my brothers."

His answer discloses the dialectical dynamic of urbanization. The villager is lured into the city by its noise and neon while at the same time he is pushed out of the village by hunger cramps and empty pockets.

When he arrives in the city, whether it be Rio de Janeiro, Leopoldville, or Bombay, he meets again the Janus face of metropolis. In Mexico City he gawks at the splendid new Reforma Boulevard; in Cairo he stands dazzled by the swank hotels along the Nile; in Tokyo he thrills to the pulsation of its electric night life. But he soon discovers that these glittering symbols of freedom and abundance were not fashioned for him. Disillusioned and embittered, he eventually finds his way to the *favela*, the *bidonville*, tar-paper shantytowns where the world's urban poor huddle together to glare at the affluent world around them and to gnaw on the bones of discontent.

The new world city is a city of hope and a city of despair. The immigrant sees for the first time that it could be different than it was in his village, but he sees that within the present scheme of things he will never taste of the milk and honey of this promised land. In the past he might finally have resigned himself to his lot, but today a new spirit stalks the *favela*. Today he sees that things can change. And he demands that things *must* change.

In India, 78 percent of those questioned in a recent poll said that sweeping changes in the economic and political system were needed, and this in a land where a few years ago, most people were content to allow the mystery of *karma* to provide them a better niche in the next incarnation. In Chile, fully 89 percent saw the need for drastic changes. The cauldrons of misery in Asia and Latin America need no cunning Communists to stir them up. They are already seething. Mobility and urbanization have supplied the revolutionary kindling; hunger and sickness add the kerosene. No spark need blow from Moscow or Peking, for such conditions in society can produce just as much spontaneous combustion as gasoline soaked rags in a suffocating attic.

Hope and despair stride hand in hand in the new world city. In India 61 percent of the urban residents questioned told interviewers they would prefer to go back to their villages if they could. But they know that what awaits them there is only stagnation, sickness, and death. With retreat cut off, the only alternatives remaining are resignation or insurrection. At the crossroads of the throbbing new cities or our new world, aspiration and bitterness collide. Out of the cities come life-giving medicines, new forms of art, the vision of life on a richer and vaster scale. Out of the same cities come the angry shriek of the beaten and oppressed and the sobs of hungry children.

The issues in this world of cities where the church lives out its mission are the same issues we find in our American cities, only multiplied a thousand times. Does unemployment in our cities deprive men of worth and dignity, casting them on the slag heap of technological abundance? In Madras only 25 percent of the working people can engage in direct productive activity. The rest sell shoestrings, beg, steal, or run an occasional errand. Restless knots of unemployed men and women gather on the streetcorners of Afro-Asian cities. But the work they need will come only when far-reaching changes are made in the economic structures of these nations, something most of their rulers have no desire to undertake.

Do we have hunger in our cities? UN officials report that today two-thirds of the human beings in the world live at or below the subsistence level. More important, however, is that the percentage of hungry people is increasing every year, not decreasing. Not only is the gap between the haves and the have-nots *within* various countries widening, but the gap *between* have and have-not nations is widening at an accelerated rate. The Swedish economist Gunnar Myrdal predicts that within a decade the world will have to cope with starvation on a scale unprecedented in recorded history. This will come, he says, because even if we sought merely to maintain present standards, we would have to double the world's food supply by 1980 and triple it by A.D. 2000. There is no indication that we are willing or able to do this. "Famine" is a faceless word. But hunger is personal. It means the reduction of man to his basest emotions. A really hungry man thinks only of food, and will do anything for food. No crime is too dastardly for a really hungry man to commit. But hunger also means political chaos and social disorganization. It means that a world writhing in discontent will experience even more convulsions.

Do we have crowded, unsafe, and dilapidated housing in our rural and urban poverty belts? In Calcutta, 79 percent of the families must live in one room. For seven out of ten urban families in India, the room they live in measures fifty square feet. That's five feet by ten feet, smaller than the average American bathroom. When we remember that eating and sleeping, dying and being born, arguing and making love must all go on within the same four walls, we cannot doubt this description of a comparable family of urban poor in Mexico City:

> The most striking things about these families are their general malaise, the rarity among them of happiness or contentment, the rarity of affection. . . . Above all where hunger and discomfort rule, there is little spare energy for the gentler, warmer, less utilitarian emotions. [In Oscar Lewis, *Five Families*, New York, 1962, p. ix.]

But poverty of the new world city is not like the old poverty. It is not like the deprivation which existed before the deprived knew there was a different way of life. This misery exists in full view of plenty and in a world where there are no technical reasons why everyone should not be fed. Today's poor die in front of showcases crammed with the fruits of the earth and they live in a world where peons and fellahin are rising to ungird the loins of the oppressors. Today's impoverished mothers know they are impoverished and they are ready to do anything to put food in their children's mouths. They are poor but they no longer accept their poverty as the decree of fate.

In the roach-infested slums of Sao Paulo, one of Latin America's most opulent cities, there lives an unmarried mother named Carolina Maria de Jesus. She scratches out a few pennies a day by collecting waste paper, but on a few sheets of this paper she laboriously writes a daily diary. She dreams of being a great poetess, and her writing in 1962 in *Child of the Dark* indicates that she has a genuine lyrical gift. When she is writing she imagines herself in a "dress of finest satin, and diamonds set shining in my black hair." But then she puts down her book, "and the smells came in through the rotting walls and rats ran over my feet. My satin turned to rags and the only things shining in my hair were lice" (p. 11).

Yet the difference between Carolina Maria de Jesus and the countless girls who once heard the story of Cinderella, is that

Carolina *knows* it could be different, that the satin dress and the clean house is within possibility. She is ready to cast her lot with the revolutionaries of Brazil because, as she writes in her diary, "Brazil needs to be led by a person who has known hunger. Hunger also is a teacher . . . those who govern our country now are those who have money, who don't know what hunger is, or pain or poverty."

It is the Carolina Maria de Jesuses by the hundreds of millions who create the explosive potential of our time. Like the Maria for whom she is named, also a girl whose marital state was questionable and whose child had to be housed in poverty, she might write:

> My soul magnifies the Lord,
> and my spirit rejoices in God my saviour . . .
> He has shown strength with his arm,
> he has scattered the proud in the imagination
>   of their hearts,
> he has put down the mighty from their thrones,
> and exalted those of low degree;
> he has filled the hungry with good things,
> and the rich he has sent empty away . . .
>                     (Luke 1:46-53, "The Magnificat")

Carolina Maria de Jesus represents the human side of the new world city. She is not only desperately poor, as were millions of mothers before her. She knows it, resents it, and is irrevocably resolved to change it. She incarnates hopes her forebears never dreamed of, resentments they never harbored, and an anger whose intensity they never felt. She dramatizes what some sociologists have called "transitional man," that person who has been awakened from the sleep of apathy but has not yet been made a part of the new world promise. She and the millions of people who share her feelings create what Gilbert Harrison calls "the most dangerous decades," the anguishing period between the time a people realizes that things *could* be different and the time things really change. These are the dangerous decades because they are fraught with disquietude and indignation. They provide the raw emotions which demagogues can fashion into self-defeating fanaticism, directionless violence, and the jingoisms of race and nation. But they also provide the only material out of which a truly livable human community can be shaped. The most dangerous decades are the years between the torpor and lethargy of Egypt and the historical responsibility of the Promised Land.

They are the dangerous decades too because there is always the temptation to go back to Egypt, and there is also the pressure to take short-cuts or to betray those who are leading the pilgrimage to freedom.

The dangerous decades are the forty years in the wilderness, and the urban revolution of our century in some ways reduplicates the first deliverance from Egyptian colonialism. The same God who broke the shackles of slavery from the bodies of the Hebrews and led them by fire and cloud into a vocation in history is still calling men and nations. He still calls them out of death into life, out of slavish subservience into mature servanthood, out of colonial dependence into responsible freedom, out of economic serfdom into self-reliance and adulthood. But between the call of God and the fulfillment of the promise there stretches the taut line of danger. As a world of cities, three billion human beings have left the Egypt of the past and are headed for the Promised Land of the future. And we are all living in the dangerous decades.

It is sometimes hard to affirm that God is present in this urban transformation, but He is. He is calling man to responsible care for his world. He is chastening those who have failed to exercise their stewardship of political power faithfully. He is casting down the mighty from their thrones and exalting those of low degree. He is taking the management of his world out of the hands of the King Farouks and putting it in the hands of the Carolina Marie de Jesus. He is chastening recreant mayors and governors by making them share their power with sharecroppers and piece workers. As the New English Bible puts it in First

Corinthians 1:28, "He has chosen things low and contemptible, mere nothings, to overthrow the existing order."

How does the church now live and serve in a world of cities? Our experience of recent years with mission in the city may provide us with the models we need. Wherever it is in the world, mission today will discard pith helmets and compounds. No longer do inner city parishes provide an interesting but deviant form of church life for America and Europe. They have now become the pilot projects for mission in the whole world. Industrial mission in Sheffield and Detroit now provides the experience for mission in the African copper belt, the steel mills of Bihar and the oil field of Venezuela.

But it is our brief experience in the black ghettos of America which will now provide the most valuable experience. In the ghettos we have learned a style of mission which provides the only viable model for mission in the vast Afro-Asian ghetto. What have we learned? We have learned that God wants his people to identify themselves unequivocally with the cry of the poor for justice now. He allows his word to be heard in the ghetto only when those who speak it share the existence of those who hear it. He has taught us that we must be willing to disappear, to see our buildings, our property and our institutional safeguards threatened and even destroyed so that an authentic link with the people can be fashioned. God has taught us that, like John the Baptist, we must decrease if he is to increase. He has taught us that in the institutional temple of religion, perhaps no stone can be left standing on another before the new temple of the body of Christ emerges. As long as we try to keep one or two stones pasted together as a possible escape route, we only succeed in postponing that indispensable identification with those whom God has sent us to serve. As we apply this lesson today it becomes evident that the antiquated separation between "home" and "foreign" missions must now be abandoned. Our mission today in Chicago or Caracas, in Los Angeles or Leopoldville, is one mission.

But what *is* the mission of the church in a world of cities? Let the names of three books of the Bible symbolize it for us.

The first is *Exodus.* Exodus is not one past event in the history of Israel. It is a permanent mark of the people of God. When the church is no longer in exodus, no longer on the way *out* of the tombs and monuments of Egypt and into the trackless wilderness, it is no longer the church. We can be thankful that in some ways the church today is on the way out of Egypt. It is leaving behind the temples of death and the relics of its cultural captivity and is marching into the desert where it learns to accept a new vocation. To be in exodus means that the church joins the march of urban man from slavery to freedom. Despite an occasional temptation to go back to Egypt, to go back to being a domesticated animal in the household of western culture, the church is on its way. It is a pilgrim people content to be on the move. Furthermore it is on the move in the company of the disinherited of this earth, moving with them toward the land of promise. This means it must say to today's major and minor Pharaohs, whether they sit in governor's mansions, mayor's offices, welfare departments, or cabinet rooms, "Let my people go!"

The second is *Psalms.* The church is called to sing and dance, to make a joyful noise and to delight in the Lord. God is calling *all* men from a dead past to a living future. This includes believers and nonbelievers, people of all races and tongues, but to church people he has given a special gift. He has given them the awareness of what he is doing and the immeasurable joy of proclaiming and celebrating it. Everyone has a part in God's drama. Men of faith have the added privilege of knowing the author, so they can thank him for what he has done, not just for us, but for everyone. So the church is a singing, as well as a marching community.

Last, the book of *Revelation.* The church knows that in reality the dangerous decades will endure until the Last Day. It cannot be content with any earthly promised land, but must constantly shove off to the next horizon. The church is a body of permanent nomads because it has a vision of a city whose maker and builder is God. In short, the church is a people who see visions. In discussing the disappearance of utopian thinking in America today, Michael Harrington, author of *The Other America*, once said, "Now, today, in the U.S.A., there doesn't seem to be any group moved by the conditions of its existence to dream." On the same note, the historian of cities, Lewis Mumford, laments, "We have not created the vivid patterns that would move men to great things."

In a world of cities, where planning, coordination, and the rational arrangement of things must increase if the world is to-continue to exist, where will there be a people "whose condition moves them to dream?" Who will provide the visionaries in a world calibrated by IBM computers? A world of cities satisfied with itself, content with its estate, a world which no longer dreams the improbable and the fantastic, is on its way to dissolution.

The book of Revelation ends with an astounding vision of a city where there "shall be no more mourning or crying or pain and where the old order has passed away." Who will keep alive the vision of this city in a world of earthly cities? The world needs visionaries because where there is no vision, the people perish.

# XI

## ⊠

# The Restoration of a Sense of Place

⊠

I want somewhere, oh somewhere,
Somewhere, O Lord,
Somewhere, oh somewhere
To lay my head.
                    —NEGRO SPIRITUAL

The woman saith unto him, Sir, I perceive that thou art
a prophet. Our fathers worshipped in this mountain; and
ye say, that in Jerusalem is the place where men ought to
worship. Jesus saith unto her, Woman, believe me, the hour
cometh when ye shall neither in this mountain, nor yet at
Jerusalem, worship the Father . . . the hour cometh, and
now is, when the true worshippers shall worship the Father
in spirit and in truth. JOHN 4:19-23.

### To Replace or Enhance

As this is written a lively discussion is raging in Boston about
what to do with the hoary old name Scollay Square now that
it is quickly being replaced by a shiny, new complex of govern-

ment buildings. Since the streets themselves have been rear-ranged and some of the actually eliminated, certain planners contend that Scollay Square simply does not exist anymore. Like the lost continent of Atlantis or that prehistoric beast called the pterodactyl, it is simply gone. They have already succeeded in getting the name of the subway station changed to "Govern-ment Center." There are churls and curmudgeons, however, who insist that simply changing the layout and architecture of a place does not abolish the place. Regional planners are not alchemists. Scollay Square, argue the traditionalists, despite its massive face-lifting, has not been vaporized. It has a right to its name.

True enough, the final years before its renewal (or elimina-tion as the case may be) were hard ones for Scollay Square. It was the favorite locus for tawdry bars, slot machine emporia, tattoo artists, and dimly lit strip joints. It was the lonely sailor's surest hunting ground and an embarrassment to the civic fathers. It is said that when its most famous building, the Old Howard Theatre, was being felled by the relentless wrecking ball, knots of men from all stations of life gathered at the site and wept. Once a legitimate theater and music hall, the Old Howard had finished its days as a burlesque house.

There can be no gainsaying the fact that in those last years before the bulldozers, Scollay Square had become a gaudy, seedy place. But still it *was* a place. It had certain character and ethos. It had a *name*. The disappearance of a sense of place, of the significance of particular spaces and locations, is one of the deplorable characteristics of our time. It is deplorable because just as our own personal identity is fixed for us in part by our feel for our own bodies and our names, our sense of identity as a society is mediated to us through the names of the places and occasions associated with the history of our people.

There is good clinical evidence to suggest that when an indi-vidual is deprived, even for a short time, of sense perception and environmental objects, he quickly loses touch with reality and degenerates into a quasicataleptic state. He becomes confused, frightened, and bewildered, unable to deal successfully with threats or challenges. This astonishingly rapid disintegration of personality has been observed, for example, in the so-called sensory deprivation laboratory of Dr. Abraham Maslow of Brandeis University. His experiments with many subjects seem to indicate that the normal functioning of personality depends on the subject's half-conscious awareness of a background of sensory items of orientation. Ordinarily, a person is not aware of this background, but when it is taken away or markedly altered, his perception of reality is dangerously undermined.

*Changes in Personality*

Naturally it is not possible under laboratory conditions to subject whole groups of people to systematic sensory deprivation or to severe alterations in their total environment. However, we are beginning to notice some disturbing changes in the behavior or groups when this happens outside the lab.

In our era of urban renewal, as whole landscapes are erased and new configurations replace them, it is important to try to understand what role the sense of space and the continuity of relationships to places plays in the life of a human group. When dozens of families are suddenly moved from a so-called slum into a high-rise housing project, the personality derangement and pathology is frequently intense. There are people who never fully recover. Likewise, I have seen in families whose homes and neighborhoods have been leveled by the urban renewal bulldozer the same symptoms Maslow describes in his subjects. I can recall quite vividly a conversation I had two years ago with one of the women who had survived the Nazi destruction of the tiny village of Lidice in Czechoslovakia. The Germans had arbitrarily picked this hamlet to be the example of what would happen to other villages if deeds like the assassination of Reinhard Heydrich recurred. They came into the town, shot all the men over twelve, then shipped the wives to one concentration camp and the children to another. They burned the village completely, destroyed all the trees and foliage, and plowed up the ground. Significantly, they demanded that on all maps of Czechoslovakia the town of

Lidice must be erased. The woman survivor confessed to me that despite the loss of her husband and the extended separation from her children, the most shocking blow of all was to return to the crest of the hill overlooking Lidice at the end of the war —and to find nothing there, not even ruins.

There is a new Lidice now, perhaps because Europeans preserve more of a sense of the importance of places and their names than we seem to. I've recently been reading *The Dog Years* (New York: Harcourt, Brace and World, 1965) by the young German author Günther Grass. His sense of the meaning of the Vistula and of places along it for the Poles and Germans who live there comes through very strongly. But the same could be said for nearly every first-rate writer. True, the names of streets are changed there, too. I was in East Berlin some years ago when the square in front of the theater used by the Berliner Ensemble was officially changed to Berthold-Brecht Platz. But when this happens the change is usually designed to enhance the historical connotations related to a place rather than to eliminate them. There is growing resistance in Germany to changing the names of streets and institutions to keep pace with political developments. Even in East Berlin I once saw a sharp cabaret satire condemning this practice. The skit poked fun mercilessly at an imaginary school in Kopenick which had been called successively the "Kaiser Wilhelm School," the "School of the Republic," the "Adolf Hitler School," the "Joseph Stalin School," and the Karl Marx School." The audience found the parody hilarious. Many of them had gotten lost, as I had more than once, by following a map made in the West on which streets in the East, now renamed for Communist heroes, were still listed with their old designations. There is something almost instinctively revolting about the Nazi and Stalinist attempts to rewrite history, a tendency which appears in the renaming syndrome.

## Not a Matter of Naming

But the sense of continuity of place necessary to people's sense of reality is not merely a matter of naming. In some ways to call a totally new place, so radically altered as to be unrecognizable, by the same name is even more disorienting. Warsaw provides an incomparable example of the symbolic role a place with a name plays for a people. When the Poles began to rebuild Warsaw, 90 percent destroyed by the Germans, they began with the ancient Stare Miastro, the "Old City," a tiny core of buildings, monuments, and churches at the center of the city. Although the Stare Miastro was not terribly useful in any practical sense, it provided an indispensable symbolic focus. The rebuilders using detailed paintings by Canaletto and referring to yellowing floor plans and drawings, reconstructed the Stare Miastro brick by brick as it had originally stood. The Germans believed they had wiped Warsaw from the map, and so did many Poles. But once the Stare Miastro was reconstituted, the rest of the enormous task of reconstruction seemed worthwhile. "Warsaw" was once again something, some *place*. Life could go on.

Let me make it clear that I have no desire whatever to be identified with those reactionaries and romantics who oppose the removal of any edifice, however dilapidated, or the construction of any new building, however necessary. I am merely suggesting that in the massive rebuilding of whole sections and cities, one of the tests of any renewal plan should be the extent to which it incorporates the continuity of those objects of visual orientation, the pre-perceptive background which provides the people of a city with form and ambience. This has to do not just with the preservation of worthwhile architectural monuments, but also with the perceptual field created by the relationships between buildings, streets, and open spaces. The acid test of any good city planner should be his capacity to detect such spatial relations and preserve them while other things are changed. To do this he will surely have to listen intently to the people who live and work in the area describing how they feel it.

There are places where this is being done. To take another example from Boston, historic Faneuil Hall, standing in a certain spatial relation to the Old Sears Crescent, has created an axis of orientation in a section of the city for generations. Wisely, the redevelopment of that area will not only preserve Faneuil Hall for its inherent interest but partially in the interest of the space it helps frame. An effort will be made to include this venerable "place" within a new series of buildings in the area. Whether the plan will succeed remains, of course, a question, but the intention is certainly commendable.

## Our Attitude toward Space

It is probably true that the present erosion of our sense of place has resulted in part from the secularization of our culture with its tendency to divest space of any sacral significance. It has arisen also from our high mobility, always accompanied by less reverence for place, and by the technological mentality of our time which allows men to rearrange the material world freely and without undue deference to some presumed inherent significance intrinsic to it.

Architecture is always one of the most reliable indices of our attitude toward space. This is noticeable first of all in our church buildings. The cathedral used to be the most prominent edifice in any city. Today, few skylines are dominated by church towers. But secularization has pushed more than just churches into the background. It has lessened our deference and awe for all authorities. Consequently, we no longer need massive public buildings to foster and express our awe. The "impulse to monumentality" has been lost. However, this should not be a matter of regret. Sir John Summerson writes in *Progressive Architecture* (June 1965, p. 144), of the things secularization has eliminated:

> The corporate or social importance of religion was one of them. The sense of the dominance of a class—of the exclusive possession of certain privileges by certain groups of people—was another. Monumentality in architecture is a form of affirmation; and affirmations are usually made by the few to impress the many.
>
> Today, the few are becoming increasingly merged in the many and there are no groups within the community

(possibly excepting the churches) who are anxious to express their corporate identities by gestures as costly and conspicuous as the erection of monumental buildings.

## Impact of the Biblical Faith

I have argued elsewhere (*The Secular City*, London: SCM Press, 1965) that this whole desacralizing and deconsecrating movement is due in large part to the impact of the biblical faith on Western culture. From the nomadic history of Israel, through the exile and the destruction of the Temple, and up to the conversation between Jesus and the woman at the well noted at the beginning of this article, the Judaeo-Christian tradition has raised sharp questions about sacral space. The holy place is always that place where God chooses to meet man, but he refuses to allow these places themselves to be sanctified. He constantly calls man away from the established holy places by speaking to him at new ones. Jesus clearly will not be drawn into a theological disputation with the Samaritan woman. He will not argue for one holy place against another, for Jerusalem against the mountain. It does not matter in which place (*topos*) man worships God, for God is a spirit, and all holy places are radically relativized by his transcendent freedom.

Two other Biblical incidents confirm this same motif. One is the story of Moses and the burning bush. God first tells him to remove his shoes, for "the ground on which you are standing is holy ground." But then he immediately orders Moses away from the holy ground and into Egypt, to lead the captives to freedom. It is clearly the mission and not the place which is central. Indeed, throughout the Old Testament, the prophets fulminate tirelessly against the "high places," those holy grottoes of Cananite worship which had been adopted in part by the Jews.

In the New Testament, the story of the Transfiguration provides a corroborative point. Here two of Jesus' disciples see a vision of Moses and Elijah, along with Jesus shining in resplendent light. The instinctive impulse of the disciples is to want to sanctify the place, to build three shrines there, one for each figure in the vision. But Jesus refuses. Just as God called Moses away from the bush, so Jesus calls his disciples away from the mountain of Transfiguration. He takes them with him down into the valley where the first thing they encounter is a maniac who runs about among the tombs.

Tombs in fact have often become the special holy places of religious devotions. So it is enormously significant that when the disciples come to Jesus' tomb to perform acts of traditional piety, they find it broken and empty. The doctrines of the Resurrection and the Ascension deal the final blow to any Christian animism, any special deference to one place more than another.

## Necessary for Humanization

The Biblical devaluation of religious space and holy places has contributed to our present sense of placelessness, but this should not be seen as a negative thing. The desacralization of space is, I believe, a necessary prelude to its humanization. It delivers man from the demons and banshees and renders the world "mere world." The earth is man's garden, his responsibility, not a fitting object of religious awe. Man is to worship God and God alone. Freed of its sacral aura, the world can now be recreated by man. This desacralization becomes negative only when its *purpose*, the liberation of man for the service of God and fellow man, is lost from sight. Space is freed from magic so man can thankfully use it and delight in it.

The process might be seen in four stages corresponding to four meanings of space and place theologically:

The first is *magical* space. Here all space and place have an ambiguous, demonic/benign character. Man cringes before the world. He is the vassal of the place spirits. He must placate them and be careful not to offend them.

The second is *sacral* space. Here the sacred places are distinguished from the secular ones. Man moves back and forth between the two. His world has holy places, loaded with terrible significance, but the world is dichotomized. The relation of the holy places to the secular ones becomes problematical.

The stage of *secularist* space comes next. Here all space is homogenized and every place becomes interchangeable with every other place. Locations, like the airports of big cities, become indistinguishable, and life becomes monochrome and lacklustre. The Scollay Squares and Elfreth's Alleys disappear in monotonous blocks of urban sameness.

Now the stage of *human* space, in which both animism and abstraction have been transcended, begins to emerge. Space is experienced neither as malevolent nor as infinitely malleable. Space is *for* man, and places are understood as giving pace, variety, and orientation to man.

### Universe as "Christic"

This understanding of the human significance of spatiality is given support by two influential theologians of our era. Karl Barth built his multi-volume *Church Dogmatics* around the central motif of the Covenant in the Bible. He contends that the Covenant actually precedes the Creation. God determines to be God-for-us and God-with-us (Emmanuel) "before the foundation of the earth." For Barth, therefore, the whole Biblical epic—the creation, the calling of Israel, the sending of Jesus, the appearance of the church—all constitute the outworking of God's determination to be *for* man. Barth's theology supplies the basis for a sweeping kind of Christian humanism. The whole world, the place where man is set, is *for* him. It is man's world, not in an abstract or vacuous way, but through the divine intentionality.

Likewise, Teilhard de Chardin emphasizes the evolution of the cosmos as a humanizing process. The world becomes more and more "Christic" and at the same time increasingly man's world. Man becomes progessively more responsible for its growth and guidance and while assuming this station he participates in the deepening and refining of his humanity. Thus, the entire cosmos is a place for man's fulfillment and enhancement.

The universe is neither malevolent nor mechanical but "Christic," i.e., the spatial dimension of God's concern for man.

The influence of Christianity on Western culture has moved it from the magical through the sacral stages of understanding space and place. But that influence will be aborted if we now settle for an abstract, geometric view of place, denuded of its human meaning. We should be very clear about what tack the church and theologians should take in moving us away from the flat and anemic sense of place which now plagues us. Some theologians are tempted to call us back to a sacral sense of space, to add variety by extolling the numinous character of the holy places. I do not myself believe this is the wisest course. I believe we should remedy the present erosion of the sense of place not by a return to sacrality but by an emphasis on the *human* significance of space.

## The Human Scale

This leads us to a very important theological issue centering on the significance of the Incarnation. It has a direct bearing on our philosophical view of space. Although Eastern theologies of the Incarnation have often interpreted it as God's effort to divinize man and sacralize the world, the Western and Augustinian tradition seems more apposite here. It views the Incarnation as the normative sign of God's irrevocable commitment to the humanization of man and his milieu. Salvation is understood not as making man into god, but as man's being saved from the false gods so that he can be a true man.

Curiously, it is an architect and city planner with a Greek background who seems to exhibit best what this kind of a theology of place might mean in the building of cities. I refer to Constantinos Doxiadis, whose dialogues with the Protestant theologian Truman Douglass have recently been published under the title *The New World of Urban Man* (New York: United Church Press, 1965). In his contribution to the dialogue, Doxiades refers to what he calls quite aptly "the human scale," as the essential dimension of any city. He means more than the fact that we usually build doors and stairways on a scale which comports with the physical dimensions of the human individual. He means that there are also certain psychological and sociological aspects of human beings which need to be taken into consideration in our building. For example, the relation between the height of buildings and the distance between them should take into account the angle of vision within which it is comfortable for a man to see the tops. If they are too high or too close, a boxed-in feeling develops. It is also possible to gauge to some extent how many visual signals can be added to a field of perception before a point of diminishing returns sets in, how high the decibel level of sound can reach before we really hear nothing. We can even begin to tell how long a street should run before a break or corner occurs so that it seems neither endless nor chopped up.

There is much more we could find out if we wanted to take the space-for-man idea seriously, with man as the crucially basic dimension. We could find it out by observing people accurately and also by questioning them carefully about their perceptions of the city and its parts, as Kevin Lynch did in *The Image of the City* (Cambridge, Mass.: M.I.T. Press, 1962).

Does this sound too much like deriving what *ought* to be from what *is*, deciding how cities *should be* constructed from how man *experiences* space? Perhaps so. In any case it does reveal a belief that man and his experience should be placed at the center of the city. But what is wrong with such a conviction? It is clearly a value assumption shared in different ways by humanists, Christians, and others. As a Protestant, coming from a tradition which has traditionally spurned most ideas of natural law, I must say that the idea of the "human scale" might provide a kind of natural law in which I could become interested.

Still, the "human scale" must in no sense be seen as changeless or unvarying. It is really a historical rather than a "natural" phenomenon, strictly speaking. All sorts of things influence and modify the way man perceives place and space.. Jean C. Rowan writing in *Progressive Architecture* (June 1965) quotes Moholy-Nagy in his *Vision in Motion* as saying that "every great period in human civilization organically creates its particular space conception." Rowan asks how the astounding technology of our day will influence our perception and appreciation of space (p. 139):

> Today, we have many spatial experiences that did not exist before. Air travel, for instance. After a jet flight among the clouds, can one be really stirred by the architectural space within the terminal building? Or, assuming that there is a church on top of a skyscraper, how will a worshipper react to it after a thrilling ride up into the sky in a glazed, exterior elevator? Is looking down 500 feet from an upper floor of a high-rise tower a greater spatial experience than looking up 100 feet at a domed ceiling? And in the not-too-distant future, when man will be floating through the vast spaces of the celestial void, how will he react to earth's puny architectural spaces, however great they might be in the traditional sense?

But even though man's feel for place, and therefore aspects of the "human scale," is changed through history, still as we rebuild our cities today, we should be more conscious that it is for men that we are rebuilding—God, as St. Paul says, "has no need of temples of wood or stone," but man does need a place in which to be a man. He needs spaces in which to live, and these spaces should be constructed with the conscious recognition that they are for man. There is nothing irreverent in this, since if the Christian gospel is correct, God himself is *for* man, for his complete humanization and fulfillment. In the new human environment we are now constructing, should we settle for anything less?

# XII

❖

## The "New Breed" in American Churches: Sources of Social Activism in American Religion

❖

FIVE YEARS AGO THE COLORLESS HUDSON CITY OF NEWBURGH, New York, flashed briefly into national attention when its city manager proclaimed a "get-tough" policy with what he called "welfare chiselers." State and national welfare officials took a dim view of his program, however, and it was quickly terminated. The town dropped once again into obscurity. But this year, Newburgh was back in the news. On May 2, 1966, the *New York Times* carried a story with the headline: "CLERICS UNITE IN ATTACK ON NEWBURGH'S COLOR LINE." There followed an account of a rent strike in the city's Negro ghetto, a protest organized and supported by a group of the town's white and Negro clergy. Despite the opposition of most of the white population, the clergy said they would continue the strike until repairs were made to the dilapidated tenements in question. If their stated reason for being involved in this action

("The church must witness to the poor, and this includes the Negro") persuaded only a minority of white churchmen to support the action, this minority was still a conscious and articulate one.

Newburgh is not an unusual city. It has simply been fated, twice in five years, to become a stage for a larger drama. Five years ago its welfare crisis disclosed a national uneasiness with welfare policies. Today the battle raging there between socially militant churchmen and such custodians of the status quo as banks and real estate institutions is part of a nationwide phenomenon: the emergence of a "New Breed" of socially activist clergy.

Churches today are facing an unprecedented institutional and theological crisis in their mission to the city. Most of their social services have been taken over by the municipal, state, and federal governments, or by secular agencies. This partial loss of function has precipitated a wrenching reappraisal of urban church strategy in America. It has also provided the occasion for the New Breed of church leaders to seize the initiative and to move the churches away from a social-service view of urban problems toward a political one.

The New Breed has brought to the fore a style of theology and a political vision that have lain dormant for some years although they have deep sources in the Christian tradition and in the American religious experience. In Buffalo, Philadelphia, Kansas City, Chicago, Oakland, and dozens of other cities, the New Breed can be found organizing welfare unions, tenants' councils, rent strikes, and school boycotts. Wherever they are at work, they have evoked opposition, both inside and outside the churches. The resulting tensions have made church politics livelier and more interesting today than they have been for decades.

In this paper I wish to examine certain of these tensions in church politics, describe the New Breed of activist churchmen, and indicate some of the theological and sociological factors operative in the situation.

# I

Although the present battle within the churches has profound theological significance, it is not debated in overtly theological terms. Rather, the debate turns on questions of church strategy and policy. The best example of this is the discussion now going on inside the churches over what they should do about poverty. The poverty question comes up in many ways: Should the church remain largely as one of the "helping agencies" and thereby continue its traditional social-service view of poverty? Should it cast its lot with nongovernmental organizers, such as Saul Alinsky, investing money, staff, and prestige in building political power for the poor? These, not the Virgin Birth or the inerrancy of Scripture, are the issues church leaders discuss most ferociously today.

Protestant church historian Martin Marty describes the two sides this way: One side says that the Christian church should be involved in the struggle of today's poor in the city and on the farm—at the side of the delinquent, the racially oppressed, the politically exploited. The other side says the church should love these people, but should not become involved in the politics of their problems. As the new strategic-theological altercation unfolds, it becomes clear that the dispute involves three principle parties. Each has a strategy, and a theology to back it. One group simply wants the church to "stay out of politics." It includes people who hold that religion should focus on a world beyond this one, on an inner or "spiritual" life separated from the political conflict—the traditional pietists. It includes others who, though they believe the church should concern itself with justice, feel that it should not squander its efforts in the shifting sand of city politics, but should concentrate on large, more universal quests.

Another group consists of the churchgoing Bourbons. They want the church to act as the custodian of property rights and the traditions of the *ancien régime*. These people regard religion as the sacred cement that binds a society to its past. They are not against the church becoming involved in controversial issues, so long as it always upholds the conservative side. This group is small but wealthy and disproportionately influential. It is linked with conservative business interests and with such reactionary religious publications as *Christian Economics*. Although it usually maintains an aura of respectability, on its right wing it shades into fanatical Birchite groups and Billy James Hargis' "Christian Crusade."

The third group, also small but growing quickly in size and influence, is the New Breed, those laymen and clergy who are bent on moving the church toward a more direct role in supporting and inducing social change.

No one knows just how large the New Breed is. Certainly it includes a sizable minority of the ministers graduated from the main interdenominational seminaries and some of the denominational ones in the past ten years; it also includes some educated laymen who have been influenced in the years since World War II by college pastors and professors of religion.

Still, the main symbol of the New Breed is the socially activist clergyman. An indication of the weight of the New Breed's impact can be seen in the radical metamorphosis the public image of the American clergyman has undergone in the past few years. A decade ago, he was often depicted in cartoons and stories as a pompous bore, a disagreeable zealot, or a genial incompetent. Although these images still persist in certain areas, the average man is now just as likely to think of nuns, priests, and ministers leading protest marches, standing in picket lines, or organizing debates on Vietnam. This change in the stereotype of the churchman has affected the minister's self-image. It separates the New Breed from the Old. Among the clergy, the clear demarcation is between those who participate directly in the political or social struggle and those who do not.

The New Breed fights its battles mainly in the city. Although there are examples of church social activism in rural areas, the major theater of operations for the New Breed remains the American city. True, ministers and priests played a major role in the dramatic strike of the Delano, California, grape workers last year.

Also, the Mississippi Delta Ministry sponsored by the National Council of Churches is perhaps the most controversial program operating under church auspices anywhere in the country. Yet the priests and ministers involved in these activities often come from urban backgrounds and hold many of the values and beliefs of the much larger group of New Breed churchmen now at work in the cities.

Spokesmen for the New Breed have in the past decade moved into key positions in churches, seminaries, and city-mission structures. This group has accepted the "political" rather than the social-service definition of the crisis of urban poverty. Its leaders sharply criticize the traditional programs of churches and mission societies. They advocate the utilization of church resources to help mobilize the poor in various types of community organizations. They speak unapologetically of the struggle for power in the city and the churches' responsibility to enter into the struggle on the side of the exploited and powerless. In Rochester, Buffalo, Chicago, and other cities they have used church funds to support Saul Alinsky or other organizers in setting up energetic programs for organizing the poor. Negro ministers who hold positions of leadership in the civil rights movement are a crucial component in the New Breed. They have helped churches form coalitions with civil rights groups, neighborhood action organizations, and political reform movements.

Some people believe that this surprising new role the churches are playing in the cities has already begun to have an important effect. Saul Alinsky said in a recent interview that the churches in the 1960's have assumed the role played by the labor unions in the 1930's. "The unions are now the haves—they're part of the status quo," says Alinsky. "The Christian churches are now taking the leadership in social change." Alinsky has worked with priests and ministers to organize the poor in the ghettos and gray areas of a dozen American cities. He has had years of experience, but he recently conceded that he has never seen the equal of the "pure flame of passion for justice you find in these young ministers today." Although he admits that large sections of the church remain inert or reactionary, he still contends that the church is often less compromised than most other large urban institutions and that, in any case, it has a gospel that "constantly forces it to think about siding with the poor," even when such a posture militates against its own institutional interests.

Since Alinsky's work exposes him mainly to the militant minority within the churches, his evaluation is undoubtedly biased. He may underestimate the strength of those elements in the church today that are more sclerotic than any fossilized labor union and far removed from the hope and hates of the urban poor. But he has spotted an important trend. There is a new mood in the churches, and it is gaining ground quickly.

The debate unleashed by the New Breed is far-reaching. It simmers just below the surface at the national meetings of denominations, church agencies, and church organizations. It often breaks out into open opposition as it often did against Eugene Carson Blake. Blake is now Secretary-General of the World Council of Churches; until May 1966 he was Stated Clerk of the United Presbyterian Church. One of the first top church officials to be arrested in a civil rights demonstration, Blake is a hero of the New Breed. In an article on the task the church currently has before it, Blake said: "The Church must identify itself much more radically with the interests of the poor, the losers, the outcasts and the alienated. . . . The mark of the presence of the awaited Messiah is still related to the poor having the gospel preached to them and the captives being released."

The debate also erupts frequently in city councils of churches. In Rochester, New York, the Council of Churches voted in 1964 to raise $100,000 to support a militant community organization among poor Negroes. The local radio station WHAM threatened to cancel the Council's weekly religious program. When the churches persisted in their plans for the community organization, they were shut off the air; the case is now before the F.C.C. The Council's executive insists that even though the church's radio voice has been silenced, the church is preaching the gospel by its identification with Rochester's dispossessed.

This argument rages in city after city and church after church. Although the fight seems at first to be about tactical considerations, it actually has profound theological overtones. It raises the most basic questions about the mission of the church, the nature of its faith, and the central problem of where men encounter God in an urban secular world.

## II

Why has a movement of militant, politically conscious churchmen emerged in American cities in the past decade? There are both sociological and theological reasons; the phenomenon cannot be understood without exploring both dimensions.

Sociologically, the emergence of the New Breed can be accounted for by the change in the distribution of power among ethnic and religious groups that has taken place, especially in the older cities of America, in recent years. A Catholic mayor and city council, who usually have close ties with the Irish, Polish, and Italian poor, have in some measure replaced the Protestant oligarchies in the city power structure. Of course, there are still many poor Catholics, but the noisy "new poor" in American cities are often Negroes and Appalachian whites, and mostly Protestants.

The sociological and political basis for the new role churches are playing in urban politics may be the common antagonism for City Hall shared by displaced middle-class white Protestants and by disinherited white and Negro poor. The coalition these groups form is sometimes strengthened by other partners: reform-minded Jews of the type who swallowed ethnic sentiment and voted against Beame and for Lindsay in New York, and "new" Catholics who are heartened by Vatican II and whose Catholicism is a matter of conviction rather than a badge of ethnic identification.

Admittedly this alliance of disparate groups is a recent one; and the connections between the parties, tenuous. Middle-class Protestants and Jews tend to have a League-of-Women-Voters mentality. On the whole, they are devoted to civic improvement, interested in constitutional reform, but suspicious of noisy, conflict-inducing community organization and of sharply partisan politics. Poor whites cooperate uneasily with the Negroes. Catholics are upset when they are accused of "betraying their kind." But however flimsy this coalition may sometimes appear, it is the expression of important social and political realities. If the coalition combines the vigor of the New Breed in the church and the energy of today's Negroes, we may be witnessing the appearance of a formidable new ingredient in the mixed stew of American urban politics. If so, it is a force that politicians will ignore to their peril.

The bureaucratization of religious organizations is the second factor contributing to the entrance of church groups into the political arena as forces to be considered. Although this may sound unlikely to some church members and even to some religious activists, there can be little real doubt that it is true. As Max Weber said, the rationalization of religions produces a group of religious specialists; these specialists then refine, restate, and clarify the beliefs and practices of the religion, often in ways that laymen disapprove. At the upper levels of governmental and private bureaucracies one sees today the development of a group of people who are in command of information and technical competence and can exert influence and leadership that goes considerably beyond the views of the people they are supposed to represent. Such professional initiators of policy populate the research staffs of many elected officials and of numerous public and quasi-public agencies. They often staff the foundations and the command posts of large voluntary associations. They can also be found on the staff of church organizations, and this raises an important question about the relations between lay and professional members in religious groups. It is especially important for many Protestant groups where an authority ostensibly flows from laity to designated officials. Despite explicit doctrines of congregational autonomy and grass-roots authority, something like a "managerial revolution" has taken place in the church. Many church leaders form and lead rather than merely reflect and represent the opinions of their constituencies.

The coming of the managerial revolution to Protestantism

means that the wrangle between the New Breed and its opponents is in no sense a battle for the freedom of laymen against a dominating clergy. It is often the reverse. Activist ministers must frequently contend with the socially conservative laymen who sit on the boards and committees that rule the churches. This is particularly important to point out in view of the vocal demands among Catholic laymen today for a wider responsibility in the governance of their church. Protestantism in America, at least in its main-line denominations, is far from being completely lay controlled, but it is often where lay control is most powerful that the social-service mentality and opposition to social action has been most vociferous. Correspondingly, where the managerial revolution has freed ministers and church executives from subservience to laymen, there is *more* of a tendency toward social involvement. Studies have shown that ministers who do not serve a local parish, and hence are somewhat more insulated from direct lay control, are much more likely to demonstrate and become involved in direct action than are pastors of local churches. Of the hundreds of clergymen who flew to Selma, a disproportionate number were denominational and interdenominational staff people, college and university chaplains, and ministers of mission churches not directly dependent on a congregation for their financial support. The same could be said for involvement in urban political issues. Ministers not directly answerable to lay constituencies are joined in New Breed activities by pastors, including Negroes, whose congregations approve their involvement. Ministers of conservative congregations in suburbs or downtown are less likely to lean toward New Breed activism. Likewise priests who belong to religious orders are more likely to take unpopular stands than are the secular priests who serve parish congregations.

Thus, the emergence of the New Breed can be understood in part from a strictly sociological perspective. It expresses a new constellation of political groupings in the American city. It springs from the bureaucratically secured freedom of church executives who have been liberated by tenure and specialization from immediate answerability to lay sentiment. But such explanations always leave much unsaid. One study shows that ministers who belong to denominations that have taken stronger stands on civil rights tend to become more deeply involved in this struggle than ministers whose national church bodies have issued weaker statements. In other words, there are religious and theological variables at work. Unless we specifically examine what Gerhard Lenski calls "the religious factor," our picture remains incomplete. Without a "religious factor," for example, it would be hard to explain why the behavior of certain Catholics conflicts markedly with ethnic and class expectations, or why church leaders urge courses of action that may threaten their class and institutional interests.

## III

Two elements in the belief systems of the churches have a direct bearing on the emergence of the New Breed. One is the "holiness of the poor," the special status assigned to the poor in Christian theology. The other is the idea of the "blessed community," the high value put on equality and personal participation in the congregation and in the society as well, especially in religious groups deriving from the English Reformation. The Negro freedom movement, particularly as it is embodied in such charismatic leaders as Martin Luther King, has often served as the vehicle through which churchmen have moved toward activism on a wider range of issues. But King's persuasiveness lies in part in his ability to appeal to values that are deeply enmeshed in the American religious tradition. The Negro becomes the present embodiment of "the poor," while "integration" points to the vision of a holy community. All this is made explicit on such ritualistic occasions as the 1963 March on Washington where the ritual culminated in King's "I Have a Dream" sermon.

It is also essential to notice that the two elements, the holy outcast *and* the blessed community, must go together. Without the vision of restored community, the holiness ascribed to the poor would fall far short of politics and result in a mere perpetuation of charity and service activities. But the two together, mediated to American theology from the classical theological tradition by the emphasis on the Kingdom of God and the Social Gospel, produce a powerful ideological stimulus without which the New Breed remains incomprehensible.

Let us look first at the place of the poor in Christian theology. Saul Alinsky is correct in saying that whatever their degree of institutional compromise, the churches have an inconvenient gospel that constantly reminds them that they should be the protagonists of the poor. This tradition has deep roots. Although the ancient Jews saw prosperity as a sign of divine favor, they also believed that God would severely judge those in power who abused the poor. This is evident, for example, in Nathan's parable to King David (II Samuel 12:1-6) and in the preaching of such eighth-century prophets as Amos, Isaiah, and Micah. The Mosaic legislation and particularly the Priestly Code make the poor—especially widows, orphans, and sojourners—objects of special solicitude (see Leviticus 5 and 19). Among the Israelites, the poor had the privilege of gleaning and the right to the produce of the land during the sabbatical year.

From the outset, the outcast has occupied a special place in Christian theology. In Jesus' teaching it is the poor who inherit the Kingdom; his recorded utterances fairly seethe with invective against the rich. Whether these sayings are really his or whether they reflect the ethos of the early church is not important for our purpose. In either case, the poor, the disenfranchised, and the underprivileged were believed to be holy; they were thought to be in some way especially favored of God.

Most early Christian congregations were made up of poor people, as Paul discloses in the opening section of his first letter to the Christians at Corinth. Passages critical of the rich may reveal, therefore, an element of *ressentiment*. Still, these ideas were fixed in canon and liturgy and have periodically exerted an important influence on the church. This is obvious when one thinks of the continuous impact that one single text, "Sell all you have and give to the poor," has had throughout church history. It was a crucial determinant in the birth of the monastic movement and the Franciscan order among others. This case and countless others demonstrate the importance of value and belief to social change.

With the rise, after Constantine, of the Medieval Catholic church and the resulting alteration in the class composition of Christianity, there was a corresponding retreat from the mystique of the poor. Although the monastic movement tried to emphasize its religious importance, poverty was eventually defined, along with celibacy and obedience, as one of the "counsels of perfection" required of the dedicated religious elite within the church but not of the vast majority of believers. The poor, both clerical and lay, were viewed as those whose presence in the society provided the needed occasion to give alms and exercise the virtue of charity. In a subtle way, the virtue seen by early Christians in the poor themselves was now transferred to those who gave to the poor.

With the coming of the Protestant Reformation and the rise of capitalism, the idea that the poor were especially dear to God temporarily lost favor. Moral strictures on the poor became common. Their failure to flourish was interpreted as evidence of the displeasure and wrath of God. Still, the value of compassion for poor people was never wholly lost, and England passed its first real poor-relief act in 1601, emphasizing work relief for able-bodied men and apprenticeships for children. But the suspicion that pauperism came mainly from sloth rather than from the inability to find a job caused relief payments to be kept lower than the wages paid to the poorest workers. In many European countries, the churches retained control of poor relief until the nineteenth century.

Throughout Western history, contempt for the poor as morally inferior people was constantly challenged by the belief in their holiness. The idea that the indigent were bearers of special virtue and religious significance was always kept alive. Roman Catholic orders stressed the value of poverty. Heretical groups such as the Waldensians, founded in 1179 by Peter Waldo as "The Poor Men of Lyons," tried to call the whole church back to apostolic poverty. Moravians and Methodists spread their doctrines at first mainly among the poor. Among modern Roman Catholics, writers such as Dorothy Day and her followers of *The Catholic Worker* kept the idea of God's presence among the poor alive in a church that was often debased and cheapened by American success standards. It is noteworthy that Michael Harrington, whose eloquent book on poverty *The Other America* (New York, 1962) made such a mark on the .American conscience, began his writing career with *The Catholic Worker*.

But this traditional emphasis on the holiness of the poor in Christian theology could not by itself have produced the New Breed. A tradition of *concern* for the poor could just as easily lead the churches today into the social-service rather than the political attitude toward poverty. The other operative theological and ethical tradition is the equalitarian vision of the blessed community in which everyone participates without distinction. Although this image recurs many times in the Bible, it is perhaps best seen in Jesus' parable of workers in the vineyard, each of whom receives the same pay although they have worked different lengths of time. This parable illustrates the radically equalitarian eschatology of Christianity, in contrast, for example, to the ancient Egyptian belief that royalty would still reign and slaves still serve in the next life. When the principle of radical equality before God and equal participation in the community is applied to the present society, and not just to the church or to the world to come, it has explosive consequences for secular polity. This belief in "participatory democracy," along with a devotion to the poor and dispossessed, supplies in one way or another the theological fuel for today's New Breed.

Where did this conviction originate? The rankless equality of participants was a central feature of the earliest Christian congregations. The Apostle Paul speaks of equality between slave and free, Greek and barbarian, and men and women. With the development of a hiararchically ordered church and the assumption by Christian priests of the *privilegien* once accorded the priests of the imperial cultus, the principle of radical equality was, however, eclipsed. Again, as in the case of poverty, it was emphasized if not always practiced by the religious orders. Some historians contend that the practice of full electoral democracy began in the West in the Benedictine monasteries.

With the Reformation, the religious equality of all was again strongly emphasized. Although the left-wing Reformers wanted to extend the idea to the entire society, Luther insisted that to confuse equality before God and equality among men was a serious error. It was in seventeenth-century England that the value of "participatory democracy" was most successfully lifted from the religious congregation alone and applied to society as a whole. In Cromwell's army "even cobblers and tinkers" were exhorted to reflect upon political problems. Thus the ideal of a society where everyone participates in politics, where no one is excluded in principle from the decision-making in the commonwealth, entered the Anglo-Saxon tradition. It is still operative today and is unquestionably one of the beliefs motivating the New Breed of churchmen.

Not only were all men called by God to political participation, according to the Puritans, but it was possible to establish certain elements of God's Kingdom here on earth. The Calvinism of the English Puritans, as Michael Walzer has shown in *The Revolution of the Saints* (Cambridge, Mass., 1965), "appropriated worldly means and usages: magistracy, legislation, warfare. The struggle for a new human community, replacing the lost Eden, was made a matter of concrete political activity."

This impulse toward the reconstruction of the political community along lines that would insure a greater realization of ethical and religious values continues to operate in our society today. When combined with a theologically grounded compassion for the poor, it produces a potent motivational factor. But it required a view of the possibilities of the outcast and his potential for political participation that had not been present during the medieval period. Puritanism supplied this missing link. As Walzer goes on to say, the Puritan program required "a recognition that all subjects were knowledgeable and active citizens, rather than naïve political children, that government was not a household, the state not an extended family, and the king not a loving father."

This same set of beliefs about man, when applied to the American scene today, results in a rejection of the social-service definition of poverty and an endorsement of the political definition. It provides the often unspoken assumption by means of which the young turks can argue that "poverty" is not merely the lack of money and of services by some people, but the failure of the political community as a whole.

## IV

With the coming of the New Breed, the American churches have begun to reclaim a central element of their past. H. Richard Niebuhr has argued that the ideal of establishing the Kingdom of God on earth is the most persistent and pervasive theme in the history of American theology. It brought many of the first settlers to a foreboding new continent. It helped inspire the founding fathers of the republic. It came to fervent expression in the nineteenth century in the Social Gospel Movement under Washington Gladden and Walter Rauschenbusch. In turn, the Social Gospel greatly influenced the social thinking of the Federal Council of Churches in its famous "social creed of the churches" of 1908. With the coming of World War I, the Social Gospel Movement, for which pacifism was a central tenet, began to lose momentum. Later it was displaced theologically by the so-called neo-orthodoxy movement. Reinhold Niebuhr, with whom neo-orthodoxy is usually associated in this country, perpetuated many of the elements of the Social Gospel, though he was often critical of what he took to be its naïveté about power.

The present renewed interest in political action for the poor among New Breed churchmen is not just a "return to the Social Gospel." It is more than that. It is a reclamation of the main stream of theology in America, a stream that was only temporarily diverted by the European existentialist theologies after

World War I. Those who see in the New Breed a mere outburst of secular activism reveal a lack of familiarity with the history of religion in America. The Kingdom of God, which in the neo-orthodox period had become an "impossible possibility," has become once again something for which to work.

Still, there are differences between the current crop of socially militant churchmen and their spiritual forebears. The views of the New Breed tend to be more provisional. They do not believe that one push will bring in the Kingdom. They tend less to identify particular utopian schemes, such as socialism or pacifism, with the gospel. They are more appreciative of secular allies and see the church more as a supporter and strengthener of movements already under way than as a vanguard. They rely less on preaching and are more willing to lead the institutional church directly into the struggle for power for the poor. The New Breed has learned its lessons from Reinhold Niebuhr and combined them with the spirit of the Social Gospel. It has renewed the quest for the Kingdom of God on earth, but it has done so with a deeper realization of the intransigence of evil and a more realistic idea of power and how it functions.

This, then, is the theological perspective of the New Breed. It underlies its claim that the social-service agencies, including those operated by the church, do little to remove poverty. According to the New Breed, these agencies merely reduce the guilt of the non-poor by fostering the illusion that "something is being done." And this illusion leaves little strength or inclination to make the structural changes necessary to close the gap between the culture of poverty and the majority. So strong is the New Breed's contempt for the Lady Bountiful attitude toward the poor that certain church agencies have advised their local congregations *against* any cooperation with the government's War on Poverty unless the programs guarantee power and participation for the poor. The April 1966 *Newsletter* of the Division of Church Strategy and Development of The United Presbyterian Church in the U.S.A. warns its readers about the War on Poverty:

There are serious dangers in the way current community action programs are being structured. Lines of control are being drawn tightly to a central bureaucracy. Vital dynamic elements in the city are in danger of being smothered by the kinds of control of the local citizens which are built into the operations of the city poverty operation. Full endorsement seems inappropriate.

Here the traditional Christian interest in the poor and their welfare has been informed by a social eschatology, a dedication to the restoration of full participation in the commonwealth. This hope for the realization of the blessed community, though expressing itself in secular political form, is, as we have seen, authentically religious in origin.

The New Breed of activist churchmen stands in the succession of Roger Williams and William Penn, both of whom sought to establish a colony of heaven on earthly soil. They witness to their faith in a style that would have been familiar to their forefathers among the Free-Soilers, Abolitionists, Feminists, and Social Gospelers. This tradition, which was partially eclipsed by a generation of church theologians heavily influenced by Europe, represents the reappearance of an authentically American religious stream. The New Breed may appear "secularized" to some, but they have an honorable religious history behind them.

What will happen to the New Breed? They will probably not succeed completely, either in their efforts to win control of the church from the Old Guard or in their attempt to abolish poverty, war, and injustice in our society. They may even grow old and complacent. But at the moment, these young activists are trying with some real success to lead the American churches away from their nostalgic dream of the rural past and into the peril and promise of an urban future. In doing so they may restore to visibility a religious tradition at least as old as the American experience itself. Even if they do not fully succeed, they are writing a fascinating chapter in the history of not only the American church, but of the republic as well.

# XIII

✣

# Where Is the Church Going
# and How Will It Get There?

✣

THE CHRISTIAN CHURCH TODAY IS UNDERGOING UNPRECEDENTED transformation, and there is hardly anyone left who is willing to dispute this. In the middle of the big change, it is not possible to gauge whether today's revolution will be more far-reaching than the one which shook the church during the sixteenth century. But I rather believe that, in the long run, it will be.

The sixteenth-century Reformation did not really push the church beyond medieval Christendom. Only the so-called left-wing sects tried to move into the newly emerging modern world, and they met severe opposition from Luther and Calvin. The sixteenth-century Reformation was mainly a reformation of the *church*. Its important impact on the society was largely indirect. Our present reformation, on the other hand, has to do more with the church's relationship to the secular order and only secondarily with its internal life.

The question, "Where is the church going?" can be answered best by saying that it is going *away* from a society in which it had to play the role of moral instructor and symbolic cement for the entire culture. It is moving now toward a new period in which the church will be a minority in Diaspora.

This new minority status certainly will relieve the church of many of the onerous tasks it has had to perform. It will also take away many privileges it enjoyed during the period of Christendom.

### The New Servant Church

• In a church on the way out of the past of Christendom and moving toward the future as a servant minority, we can expect to see the development of more distinctive *Christian styles* of life. I say *styles* in the plural because I believe Christians will not have a single style of life, but rather a large number of variations and substyles. Some of these substyles probably will be described as "incognito Christianity," not visible to the world in any particularly distinctive way.

Let me list some of the characteristics of one of the new Christian styles which I think probably will appear.

Its first characteristic is what we now begin to call *Christian presence*. This word presence comes originally from the French Roman Catholic personalist tradition in theology. It designates the determination of the church to share in the suffering, sacrifice, pain, and conflict that mark the society.

In France, for example, there is an organization of lay Christians called CIMADE. This group is made up of people who have accepted the discipline of going to those places where there is social conflict, racial turmoil, war, revolution, or natural disasters. Once on the scene, they live there for months, or years if necessary. This idea of simply *being present*, as men who live among men, is a corrective to the image of the church as moral instructor or proselyter. It has become influential in the thinking of the student Christian movement, where presence is seen as the main function of the church in the university.

Second, a certain amount of *verbal reticence* will certainly characterize the future style of Christians. The church has been seen by those outside its life too much as a talking and preaching organization. For many people, "church" means the place where one hears long boring disquisitions or is hectored about one's moral failings or is asked for money. Church people are thought of as those who are fully equipped with quick and easy answers to questions no one is asking.

By verbal reticence, I do not mean some kind of Zen Buddhist esoteric aphorisms. The Christian gospel is inextricably related to the *Word*, and it is not possible to communicate it fully in mere silent action or living testimony. However, the Word comes only in situations of authentic human communication. And human communication comes as a result of one's being willing to listen to the other, to live with him, and to respond only when there is some indication of interest. Perhaps what the church needs to do as it moves from past to future is to win back its right to be heard, to place itself once again in the position where people may ask why Christians do the things they do.

Third, the church of the future certainly will have an important *political dimension*. We are discovering that renewal of the church happens only when the church resumes political apostolate. Whether we look at the East Harlem Protestant Parish, the Iona Community in Scotland, the worker-priests of France, or the Roman Catholic revolutionaries in Latin America, wherever we find new life in the church we find political engagement. Future church historians will certainly notice that the major religious figures of our era, the saints of the twentieth century, achieved their sainthood mainly in political obedience.

During the next months and years it will be impossible to separate political obedience from a new form of Christian apostolicity. Our main problem in the church will be how to become politically engaged without being arrogant crusaders. Frequently in the past we have refused the role of political partisanship because it has led to a crusading spirit. No one, however, has ever proved that political partisanship *necessarily* produces this kind of arrogance. We need to be *both* specific and humble in our political obedience.

F

## Beyond Denominations

A much more difficult question is *how* the church should get from where it is to where it wants to go. Certainly, denominations have long outlived their usefulness and now provide more of a barrier than a help to mission in the world. The disputes between Presbyterians and Methodists are as relevant to mission in the modern metropolis as are the squabbles between the "big-enders" and the "little enders" in Swift's *Gulliver's Travels*.

But the real issue is how to get from denominations to the ecumenical church. Certainly we do not get there merely through high-flown church-unity consultations or mergers of churches at the national level. What we need is the kind of grass-roots ecumenism in which people work together in their own local communities on issues that Christians need to confront together, without reference to denominational lines. This means the organization of *ad hoc* congregations drawn from people who represent various religious and denominational backgrounds. It calls for a regrouping around the points of pain and possibility in the modern world itself.

We need congregations who will study, worship, and work together on the issue of housing or education or racial justice or urban transport or mass media or sex and family ethics or youth questions.

We need congregations who will be mobile; congregations led by laymen with the help of theologically trained persons; congregations who will devise ways of acting and praying together—ways still unheard of in our doomed denominational Christianity.

In a "manifesto" published two years ago in *Renewal* magazine, Stephen Rose recommends that the denominations see themselves in the future as research and development agencies serving the whole ecumenical church. He claims, rightly, that if denominations were shorn of many of their current institutional functions, they would be free to concentrate on pilot projects, on *ad hoc* experimentation, and on creative ecumenical projects on the national and international level. On the local level we would reorganize the church around metropolitan areas; pooling resources, talent, and personnel to address ourselves to the issues of the metropolis.

The main question, which emerges as we discuss how to move the church from denominational imprisonment toward freedom for service in the world, is what individual Christians should do with the churches in which they are now involved as members, or even as ministers. This question cannot be answered for everyone in a general way. Some have removed themselves from their congregations and denominations. On the other hand, there are people who plead for renewal and reconstruction of existing forms of church life by trimming here, consolidating there, and deepening further the points at which renewal is beginning to appear in the institutions themselves.

## Two Possible Ways

What should we do? There is no way to resolve this dilemma except to say that every Christian intent on renewal of the church for its service in the world must face his own responsibilities, and the possibilities in the congregation and denomination of which he is a part. For some the answer may be to withdraw; for others it may be to continue to fight from within. Both of these individuals, however, stand in need of a sustaining congregation where they can correct, support, and criticize each other, where they can lick their wounds, and where they can speak and dream about their hopes for a new society and a new church. This will require the development of groups which include both those who are alienated from contemporary church structures and those who are still at work within them.

The forces of renewal in the church would be irresponsible if they were to abandon all hope for the reformation of its present structures. No one can tell whether a given institutional expression of church life can be renewed or not. This often takes a long time to determine. Those who have chosen to work outside existing institutional structures, however, need not feel guilty that they are not spending their lives renewing church institutions. In short, this is a matter of vocation. The church of the future will emerge at the edges of the existing church. It will include many who are within it and many who now are not. It will exhibit certain transfigured structures of today's church as well as completely novel forms of church life which we have not yet even imagined.

It is encouraging to notice that some people with a commitment to renewal have made the hard choice to work within a church hierarchy, city-mission society, denominational headquarters, local-church pastorate, or as a layman functioning at any one of these levels. These people deserve our support and encouragement and should not be criticized merely because they have made this choice. However, it is important to ask them in love and in concern whether their hope for the renewal of the church can really be realized within their present commitment.

Similar questions should be raised with those who make the choice to leave existing institutional forms of the church to live on the love and support made available to them by small house churches and Bible-study and discussion groups, industrial mission groups, student Christian-movement cells, and other similar groups. These people should be asked occasionally whether their decision to pull out of the church is still a valid one, and whether their zeal for renewal might help influence changes in the larger structure itself.

## Pressure—A Valid Tool

Another necessary technique in the renewal of the institutional churches is the formation of what might be called political parties within the church itself. It is curious that many Christians, although they are proud of their toughness and realism about the conflict and power in the world, frequently overlook the operation of the same factors within the church.

In at least three cities in the United States, groups of young laymen and ministers across denominational lines have formed what in effect are pressure groups within the church. They exchange information on issues facing conferences and synods, the possible candidates for executive positions, and crucial decisions about program. They then help each other to exert the kind of pressure that will bring about the decisions they hope for. It is amazing to see how much can be accomplished if even a relatively small group of people become articulate, self-conscious, and willing to exercise power within the structures of church life.

Finally, the most important point to make about the renewal of the church today is that renewal is ultimately God's doing, not man's. We often become anxious and panicky about the state of the church and our hopes for its renewal without recognizing that we are powerless to renew the life of the church. For its life is a gift which comes to us from God himself.

It is also true that a fixation of interest on the renewal of the church can defeat that very objective, because God's main intention is not the renewal of the church but the renewal of the world. Therefore, our interest in the renewal of the church must be a secondary one. Our main focus of concern should be the restoration of man to his manhood, the restoration of community, and the reconstruction of the bent world to a fully human place.

If we devote our energies to this humanizing mission, we are directly engaged in the work of God, and he will take care of the renewing of the life of his people.

# ADDENDUM

## THE STATUTE OF LIMITATIONS
## ON NAZI CRIMES

# The Statute of Limitations
## on Nazi Crimes
## A Theological and Ethical
## Analysis

THE CONSCIENCE OF WESTERN MAN IS ILL AT EASE OVER THE WAR
crimes of the Nazis. We all know, somehow, that Dachau and
Theresienstadt symbolize the most grievous failure of the so-
called "Christian West" in its two millenia of history. Many
Christians remain still somewhat bewildered and defensive about
that history, and our unresolved feelings often assume the form
of self-righteous preachments or subtle attempts to sweep it all
under the rug. It was doubtful, therefore, that the West German government, when it announced in November 1964 that
it would not extend the twenty-year statute of limitations for
Nazi war criminals, expected such an avalanche of world criticism.
The decision meant that some of the war criminals would escape trial. The intense discussion which took place during the
next four months ranged over a wide variety of legal, moral,
and even theological issues. Aspects of the debate are still going

on, for our feelings about the Nazi crimes run deep, even two decades after the end of the Second World War.

The issue of the statute of limitations itself was settled, temporarily at least, when the West German Parliament voted on March 25, 1965, to extend the limitations until December 31, 1969, twenty years after the new West German Republic was given its first measure of sovereignty by the Allied Occupation Powers. This decision was welcomed by some but interpreted by others, including many Jewish leaders, as wholly insufficient. In any case, this resolution left wholly unresolved a large number of deeper and more universal issues. They are issues which apply not only to Germany but to every nation. In particular there are obvious parallels between many of the arguments expressed in the German statute of limitations debate and those expressed about the racial crisis in the United States. The following is an account of the German statute-of-limitations discussion and a reminder of the unanswered questions it leaves for Americans and indeed for everyone.

### Many Nazis Have Been Convicted—Many Remain Still at Large

In 1958 the West German Government established a special agency called the Zentrale Stelle der Landes-Justizverwaltung whose sole task was to intensify the search for those Nazi criminals who had so far escaped detection. The agency is located in Ludwigsburg and has a capable, dedicated staff. Through its efforts, combined with the work done before it was established, 5445 Germans have been convicted and sentenced since 1945 in connection with crimes committed during the Nazi period. In addition the center in Ludwigsburg has turned up information on 7000 additional suspects whose cases will be coming up eventually in German courts.

But many people believe there are still hundreds and perhaps thousands of war criminals still at large in Germany, many living under assumed names. Dr. Robert M. W. Kempner, a former Deputy Prosecutor in the Nuremberg War Crimes Trials (conducted by an Allied Military Tribunal) has estimated that there are about 27,000 potential defendants. (Of these about 16,000 worked with concentration camps; 5000 belonged to the special SS units charged with exterminating Jews; another 6000 held responsible positions in the SS or Gestapo.) Allowing for the normal number who would have died since then and sub-tracting those who have been tried, some observers put the number still to be prosecuted at over 6000. (*Digest on Germany and Austria*, German and Austrian Claims Information Office, 515 Park Ave., New York 22, N.Y., January 30, 1965, p. 6.)

Despite the fact that so much work still seemed needed, West Germany announced in November 1964 that for constitutional reasons it would not extend the statute of limitations on prose-cuting the undetected criminals. The time was due to expire on May 8, 1965, which is the twentieth anniversary of the collapse of the National Socialist regime.

Almost immediately objections were raised all around the world, but especially in Israel and in the U.S.A. In November, shortly after the German announcement, West German Foreign Minister Gerhard Schroeder came to the United States for an official visit. Representatives of the major American Jewish groups used the occasion to express in very forcible terms their view that West Germany had the moral obligation to extend the statute of limitations so that every Nazi criminal could be tracked down and tried. They pointed out that Belgium, Poland, and the U.S.S.R. had all taken action to extend the statute of limi-tations in war crimes cases so as not to bar prosecution within their jurisdiction. They suggested that West Germany "as the scene of the horror in the past and as an ally of the free world in the present, can hardly afford to do less." They indicated that many people would view Germany's decision in this matter as a kind of test of its moral seriousness in dealing effectively with its past and with the Nazis still at large within its borders.

In his reply to the American Jewish leaders, Mr. Schroeder spoke of the very large number of people, some 12,882, who had already been brought to trial. He pointed out that the expiration of the statute of limitations on May 8, 1965, would in no way prevent prosecution of all those against whom some preliminary form of indictment has been brought, even if their formal trials begin after the cut-off date. He therefore concluded that it was "very unlikely" that any "substantial number" of hitherto unknown Nazi criminals would be discovered in the future.

### Ex post facto *Legislation and the Rule of Law*

Other German officials gave additional reasons why the statute of limitations should not be extended. Some pointed out, for example, that during the Nazi period Hitler and his henchmen had violated the "rule of law" and had thrived on *ex post facto* legislation, statutes which punish people for things which were not illegal before the law was passed. They argued that people had developed a cynical view of the legal process and that today's Germany, in its strenuous effort to overcome the Nazi legacy, needed to adhere strictly to the rule of law. Extending the statute, they argued, would subvert law to other considerations and would set a bad precedent.

But critics of the German decision were not satisfied. On January 14, 1965, Jewish groups in fifteen cities across the United States cooperated with other groups in the peaceful picketing of German consulates. The demonstrations were designed to focus public attention on the moral aspects of the statute of limitations question. In almost all cases the pickets were cordially received by the various consulates. While most Consuls tried to support their government's policy, some were openly critical of it and one even conceded that he would have liked to join the picket line. It was clear from the cooperation of many non-Jewish groups in the picketing that there was wide sentiment in America in favor of extending the statute.

There is little doubt that these demonstrations, together with expressions of opinion in Israel and in other countries, had a telling effect in Germany. Within a few days German Ambassador Heinrich Knappstein requested a meeting with the presidents of the major American Jewish organizations. The meeting was held on January 27 in New York. After members of the group had reviewed the correspondence with Foreign Minister Schroeder, the Ambassador told them that he welcomed meeting them as a contribution to the removal of the wall which now stands between Jews and Germans. Although he conceded that he did not agree personally with his government's policy in this regard, he said he felt that the policy had been motivated solely by a desire to maintain a rule of law. He further suggested that the continuation of protest demonstrations would make it difficult for the German Cabinet to reconsider its refusal to extend the statute.

In complaining about the demonstrations, the Ambassador was echoing a sentiment which was also apparently strongly felt in Germany itself. In fact German Justice Minister Ewald Bucher had stated just a few days before:

> It should not be overlooked that these demonstrations were organized by Jewish organizations predominantly. These demonstrations can give support to a latent anti-Semitism in the world, since anti-Semitism is not a German characteristic alone. We have to state that we shall decide on this question with our own responsibility and not under pressure. [Quoted from Der Spiegel in Memo, National Community Relations Advisory Council, February 3, 1965.]

In the New York Times of January 19, 1965, Mr. Bucher is further reported to have spoken out sharply against "foreign interference." Referring to demonstrations in Israel and the United States he is reported to have said: "It is out of the question that the federal republic will allow itself to be put under pressure by Israel or any other country."

He went on to say that West Germany must stick to the letter of the law "even if it means living with some murderers among us."

But by this time public opinion in the United States was beginning to crystallize against the German refusal to extend the statute of limitations. On Thursday, January 28 an editorial in the *New York Times* put it on record as follows: "The decision of the West German Government against extending the statute of limitations for punishment of war criminals is most unfortunate."

The editorial then suggested that West Germany could easily extend the statute without doing violence to constitutional procedure since it did not even become a state until 1949 and did not receive full sovereignty until 1955. It suggested that by declaring 1955 as the base date for calculating legal immunity, the constitutional problem could be solved. "Few of the main participants in the Third Reich's brutalities are likely to survive another decade," The *Times* concluded. "Ten more years is not a long period for Germans to continue to accept the responsibility to remember, find and punish those who remain."

What neither Schroeder nor Knappstein mentioned in public of course is that the question of extending the statute of limitations had also become a very hot political issue within Germany itself. It was an election year in Germany. The ruling Christian Democratic Union (CDU), of which Ludwig Erhard was then leader, had not fared as well as its supporters had hoped it would after Erhard replaced the aging Konrad Adenauer. Erhard had made a series of bungles. One of his worst was the manner in which West Germany came to recognize Israel, partially, so it seemed in retaliation for Egypt's playing host to East Germany's Walter Ulbricht. Thus, to many who have long urged the Germans to recognize Israel, Erhard seemed to be doing the right thing for the wrong reason and lost prestige on every side. Most political observers agreed that the affair could scarcely have been handled more ineptly. *Viewpoint*, which is published each month by the National Council of Young Israel, editorialized on March 31, 1965:

> . . . the Bonn government having been rebuked and embarrassed by Nasser finally decided to recognize Israel as a State. Finding ourselves between Passover and Purim we are forced to note that this was not done *out of love for*

*Mordecai but rather out of hatred for Haman.* The Bonn government recognized Israel only because the Egyptian government is threatening to recognize East Germany [page 4].

## Most Germans Do Not Wish to Be Reminded of Nazi Crimes

Among Germans, relations with Israel are necessarily tied to feelings about the Jews. And it is clear that most Germans do not wish to be reminded of the Nazi crimes against the Jews, and German politicians know this. A survey conducted toward the end of 1964 indicated that 63 percent of all German men and fully 76 percent of all German women believe the prosecutions should be stopped immediately.

Finally however on March 25, the West German Parliament did vote to extend the time within which prosecutions could be started until December 31, 1969. Both the CDU and the Social Democrats voted for the decision, with only the Free Democratic Party and a smattering of CDU and Socialist deputies opposing it. It is clear that Herr Bucher, whose Free Democratic Party is strongly nationalist in style, intended to make full political use of the Parliament's decision, made against his recommendation, to extend the statute four years. He resigned immediately after the decision was made. A few days after the decision Chancellor Erhard told Dr. Joachim Prinz, head of the American Jewish Congress, that there was reason to hope that the statute might be extended still further and that a new criminal code now being prepared might eliminate all statutes of limitations for murder.

Response to the German decision was mixed. Many people, while grateful that the limit had been extended, were greatly disappointed that the additional time allowed was so short. *Viewpoint* branded it ". . . the weakest, most incipient and insulting bill" (March 31, 1965, p. 4). Marcus Greenberg, chairman of the Commission on International Affairs, American Jewish Congress, called it ". . . a scandalous affront to millions of men, women and children, destroyed by the Hitler regime." An Israeli,

Dr. Arier Kubory, chairman of Yad Vashem, called it ". . . too little and too late."

Many Germans, on the other hand, felt that their government had been brazenly pressured into the decision and were openly cynical about it. Shortly after the decision to extend the statutory deadline, a German television commentator said: "I should like to express the thanks of the German people to the members of the Parliament for the high level of the debate, and to the peopl of Tel Aviv and New York who made it possible" (*New York Times*, March 31, 1965).

Thus the disputed decision itself had been made, for the time being at least. But the discussion did not stop. The debate had opened too many issues which could not be answered so easily.

### THE NEED TO ROOT OUT ANTI-SEMITISM ONCE AND FOR ALL TIME

One of the most serious questions left unanswered by the German discussion is, of course, what is the source of anti-Semitism? How does it arise? What does it feed on? How can it be rooted out of a society? Even those most strongly in favor of extending the statute of limitations agreed that the real problem goes much, much deeper than merely apprehending and punishing Nazi criminals. The real problem is what motivated these atrocities to begin with, and how such warped attitudes can be changed.

But to raise the question of the roots of anti-Semitism, is to tread on dangerous ground, for it means that we must face the discomfiting question of the Christian sources of anti-Semitism. In his widely discussed book, *The Teaching of Contempt* (New York: Holt, Rinehart and Winston, 1964), Jules Isaac contends that, although there was a certain amount of anti-Semitism before Christianity, it tended to be sporadic and unfocused. But when Christianity came into the world, anti-Semitism was provided with a respectable ideology and has fed on it for nearly two thousand years. In comparison to pagan attacks on Jews, says Isaac, "Christian anti-Semitism, which is essentially theological, has been infinitely more pernicious and persistent . . . " (p. 32). The three main themes around which Christian anti-Semitism has clustered, says Isaac, are: (a) the dispersion of the Jews as a providential punishment; (b) the degenerate state of Judaism at the time of Jesus; and (c) the crime of deicide.

Among Christians, such scholars as Helmut Gollwitzer, Protestant theologian at the Free University of Berlin, have pointed out the various ways in which Christian theology has often fed anti-Semitism. (Gollwitzer's ideas, together with comments by several other Christian and Jewish theologians, were published in a book entitled *Der Ungekundigte Bund* [Stuttgart: Kreuz Verlag, 1962] edited by Dietrich Goldschmidt and Hans-Joachim Kraus.) Speaking at a conference at the Ecumenical Institute at Bossey on "The Church and Israel," Dr. R. Martin-Achard, professor of Old Testament and dean of the theological faculty of the University of Geneva, said:

> When the question of the Jews arises, the Church cannot ignore the fact of the burden, the very heavy burden, of responsibility that is hers for their suffering and their age-long agony. Her first gesture towards them must be to ask forgiveness. Anti-Semitism has found in Christianity strange accomplices, and . . . it is not even yet dead in the hearts of those who profess to follow Christ . . . . [Study Encounter, Study Bulletin, Vol. X, No. 2, World Council of Churches, Geneva].

Martin Niemoller has insisted for many years that until the German church formally and openly repents for its role in the Nazi period, no national repentance in Germany is possible. The fact is that something of a confession of guilt on the part of the churches was made twenty years ago in Stuttgart, just at the end of the war, by the Protestant Church of Germany. At that time German Protestants confessed that they bore some of the guilt of Hitler's crimes, "for not having protested more courageously, prayed more faithfully, believed more joyfully and loved more ardently. . . . "

But what has really come of this twenty-year old confession? Niemoller and others contend that it has meant almost nothing. Recently the same church asked itself at its meeting in Berlin, "Have we seriously endeavored to make good . . . the injustices we inflicted on other peoples and races. . . . Have we eradicated the attitude through which the rule of injustice in Germany had been made possible. . . ? (*Religious News Service*, April 12, 1965).

This is a promising sign of the German Protestant Church's recognition of its implication in the crimes of the Nazis. Yet despite this sentiment, outside a small circle of theologians who are rethinking Christianity's contribution to anti-Semitism there has been little sign of such repentance. In fact, when Rolf Hochhuth, a German Christian dramatist, wrote his controversial play *The Deputy* and dared to suggest the passive complicity of one church with the Nazi regime, churchmen of all denominations sharply criticized Hochhuth. Otto Dibelius, the Protestant Bishop of Berlin called the play "a disservice to our church and to our people." Legitimate questions might be raised about the play, but regardless of its merits, the disproportionately hysterical opposition it elicited demonstrated in part the defensiveness Christians feel on this subject.

## ALL CHRISTIANS NEED TO BE INVOLVED

But the task of challenging ancient and unexamined attitudes within Christianity does not belong only to the German Christians. All men must search their consciences. Certainly Christians must ask themselves: where are those points at which the Christian tradition, either explicitly or implicitly, perpetuates and even encourages anti-Semitism? Where in preaching, theologizing, church education are negative attitudes toward Jews openly or subtly conveyed? Until Christian churches in Germany and the United States and everywhere decide to do something about this scandal, the decision about the extension of the statute of limitations, as important as it is, remains a minor one in comparison.

## THE COLLECTIVE RESPONSIBILITY OF THE GERMANS

Another remaining question centers on the relative guilt of those who held secondary or subservient positions in the Nazi system, such as the nurses who administered lethal doses of poison to patients at the orders of physicians. There is even the question about those who, although they did nothing overtly to participate with the Nazis, nevertheless did not oppose them openly. How does the continued search for Nazi criminals touch these passive accessories? This brings up the further question of the possibility of a whole people's sharing in some kind of "collective guilt." One German once told me that if everyone who shared any of the blame for the Nazi crimes were behind bars today, only a small minority would still be on the outside. What can the courts of any nation do in such a situation (especially when the courts themselves still contain many jurists who sympathized with the Nazis)?

This is a touchy question to answer, but in addition, since in a sense Germany itself is more or less on trial, it presents the dilemma of the ethical legitimacy of asking the present generation to pay for the trespasses of a former generation.

Ambassador Knappstein in referring to this subject, told the Jewish leaders in New York that he did not accept the idea of collective guilt but that he did accept the idea of "collective shame." This is a curious statement. Why should anyone be ashamed of something for which he bears no responsibility? The question remains, is collective guilt of any sort a possibility?

There has been a decided tendency among modern liberals and intellectuals to reject the whole idea of collective guilt as barbaric and superstitious. Responding to some of the attacks by African delegates to the UN on the Belgian-American "rescue mission" to the Congo in December 1964, Foreign Minister Paul-Henri Spaak of Belgium said:

> My sincere belief is that there is no such thing as a guilty race. My sincere belief is that there is no such thing as a guilty people. My sincere belief is that there are only mis-

guided men and contemptible men. Hitler was a contemptible man. I am sorry to say that Gbenye (leader of the Congolese rebels) is a contemptible man.

Those who argue against collective guilt even have certain clear evidences in the Scriptures in their favor. The eighteenth chapter of the Prophet Ezekiel contains one of the strongest arguments against punishing or rewarding offspring for the sins of their fathers, a matter we shall turn to in a moment. Abraham protested against God's punishing Sodom for the sins of some of its residents (Genesis 18:22). David asked God not to punish all of Jerusalem for his personal disobedience (I Chronicles 21:16-17). The well-known political scientist Louis Halle says: "The concept of collective guilt represents the substitution by childlike minds of a conceptual abstraction, in the form of a mythical collective person, for the real men, women and children of flesh and blood" (*Encounter*, April 1965, p. 62).

Mr. Halle goes on to argue that if we reject the Germans' collective condemnation of all Jews, then we must certainly reject the collective condemnation of all Germans.

It is doubtful that anyone wishes to defend the idea of collective guilt which Halle and intelligent moderns like him reject. No one seriously claims that *all* Germans are equally guilty of war crimes. Is there, however, a sense in which, just as man is by his very nature a *social* being, so his greatness in guilt is also in some real sense social? No one will deny that the SS Troopers and Gestapo officials were themselves fully responsible for the pain, death, and humiliation they inflicted on countless victims. In a larger sense, however, their parents, schools, churches, and their cultural leaders share that responsibility. This wider circle of persons not only taught the SS to hate, directly and indirectly, but also provided the atmosphere in which they were able to carry out their heinous crimes. In addition, the whole family of nations shares responsibility for having allowed Germany to follow the course it did and, similarly, for having provided an international atmosphere in which the Nazis were permitted to carry out their crimes.

Guilt is never individualistic. It is always to some degree corporate, but this raises the question of how a whole society, or indeed a whole civilization repents and starts over. Certainly the Nazi period amounts to a massive self-invalidation of Christianity. The fact that Nazism developed in the land which cradled the Reformation and provided the leadership in Protestant theology for centuries is of more than passing interest. Yet the fact that the whole of western civilization is involved in the guild of Buchenwald does not in any sense lessen the specific culpability of those who actually turned on the gas, piled up the shoes, and shoved the bodies into the ovens.

## The Forms of Corporate Repentance

The possibility of corporate or social guilt has raised in Germany the even more subtle question of what form some kind of social or corporate repentence would take. Would it take political form, involving a new relationship between Germany and its neighbor states, especially those in Eastern Europe? The failure of West Germany to extend diplomatic recognition to most of these nations (both because there are some unresolved territorial issues and because the Communist states recognize the East German regime, which Bonn sees as sufficient reason to bar the recognition of any country) is branded by some German critics as "Unbussfertigkeit" (the "Unwillingness to repent").

Or, if "social repentance" is possible, should it take some other form, cultural, social or economic, for example? Certainly most would agree that the mere payment of financial reparations is wholly insufficient. Some critics of Germany claim that only a thorough-going change in the whole economic structure of Germany will suffice to prove its penitent spirit and to prevent further fascist outbreaks. These critics, among whom are the Marxists of various varieties, point to the profound economic changes the U.S.A. forced on Japan as a precondition of democracy (i.e., breaking up the huge estates, and the like). They remind us that nothing of the kind was done to Germany. In any case, the whole problem of the relation of economic institutions to national attitudes and values remains a perplexing one. It is especially trying in Germany because some Germans rather will concede the "guilt" of "Deutschland" as such, but somehow manage to except themselves. "Collective" guilt can become a dodge for individuals.

## THE PAST IS CONTAINED IN THE PRESENT

A problem analagous to the corporate guilt question but in some ways even more elusive is that of the relationship between the crimes of the fathers and the punishment of the sons. True, those being tracked down and arrested in West Germany for Nazi crimes are those who actually committed them. But many Germans who were not involved, including many who were not even born at the time, feel that they are being punished too. On March 21, 1965, the *New York Times* carried a dispatch from Bonn which reported: "West Germans recoil from the repetitive trials today because they feel that the new Germany is being made to pay for the sins of the old."

This attitude is a familiar one to all of us. We all resent being punished, even indirectly, for something someone else did, especially if he did it before we were even born.

Yet might it be possible that here too our excessive individualism has deceived us? How can we escape the fact that we *do* profit from the investments and suffer from the lapses of our elders? We ordinarily accept the houses and bank accounts our parents bequeath to us without asking much about how they acquired them. We also usually accept many of the customs, attitudes, values, and ideas they gave to us. We live for the most part within social institutions and cultural patterns created before we were born, and most of us take little thought about how they might be changed. Thus the sharp discontinuity we often pretend to see between the past and the present is a fiction. The past is present now and continues in some ways to shape the contours of the present. It is not an authentic attitude toward the past either to sweep it under the rug or to allow it to determine our present action. Our freedom for the present arises from our having dealt successfully with our individual and collective pasts.

No one can wash his hands of history by claiming that he was not there when it was made any more than he can avoid living in houses, driving on streets or speaking a language which other people brought into being for him. If we benefit from the gifts the past bestows upon us, we can hardly abdicate from the responsibilities to which it summons us.

## THE CRIME OF THE NAZIS—GENOCIDE— IS WORSE THAN MURDER

To what extent did the Nazi crimes differ from other crimes? Many of the arguments supporting the extension of the statute of limitations pointed out rightly that these offenses were not ordinary ones. The Nazis were guilty not just of murder, the charge under which they are tried according to a German law enacted in 1871, but of crimes against humanity. We have coined the neologism "genocide" to describe a crime new to our era, the murder of a whole group of people. But such a technical word somehow masks the unspeakable horror involved in the calculated extermination of seven million men, women and children. It is often said that this was a crime without parallel in history. This is true, but we might ask whether there are other crimes, either committed or contemplated, which come near to paralleling the Nazi crimes.

What about the American bombing of Dresden, for example? Some have estimated that as many as two hundred thousand men, women, and children, mostly defenseless civilians, were killed in that raid, which took place in February 1945 and had no real military justification. In the raid on Dresden, by the careful placement of incendiary bombs, the American airmen consciously created a "fire-storm," a phenomenon which had occurred inadvertently during previous raids but had never been brought about on purpose before. A fire storm creates such a tremendous heat pocket that the oxygen in the air is sucked out. The result was that thousands of the civilians in Dresden were suffocated to death. Witnesses have reported that people attempting to flee the area were machine-gunned by low-flying American planes. Did this raid approach genocide?

One could ask about the murder of 7000 Polish officers in the Katyn Forest (probably by the Russians), the atomic bombing of Hiroshima and Nagasaki, the mass murder of Kulaks in the U.S.S.R. in the 1930's and landlords in China in the 1950's. Although so far hydrogen weapons have not been used against human beings, would their use parallel Buchenwald and Dachau? What about the use of napalm bombs and crop poisons in Vietnam?

The point here is in no way to minimize the unprecedented horror of the death camps. Rather it is to suggest that the idea of the mass extermination of groups of persons against whom we have some prejudice or with whom we have some disagreement, either major or trivial, is still very much with us. It reached its summit at Dachau, but it has been practiced on a smaller scale in many other instances.

## ALL MEN ARE ACCOUNTABLE

The important thing to notice here is that by punishing Nazis for their crimes, we are implicitly agreeing that we too must be held accountable for our deeds, and for allowing others to do things in our name. The favorite defense used by Nazi criminals is that they had no way of challenging decisions made by those above them and that they were merely following orders. If anything they are more accurate in claiming that they could do little to effect top policy than we would be if we gave the same excuse today. After all, they did live in a totalitarian state, and we live in a democracy. Nevertheless, the courts have held that these Germans were responsible for the things they did, even when they were obeying orders. By condemning them, and suggesting that the much larger number of people who permitted this to go on without opposing it bear a part of the responsibility, we are saying in effect that future generations must hold *us* responsible for napalm in Vietnam and the stock-piling of hydrogen weapons. Are we willing to accept this tit-for-tat responsibility as we insist on the continued trials of Germans?

## THE MORALITY OF ANY STATUTE OF LIMITATIONS

Another question raised by this discussion is that of the real purpose of a statute of limitations, the question of legal safeguards as such. Legal scholars say that no system of jurisprudence allows an unlimited time after a crime during which a person can be tried for it. This arises both from *practical* and from *moral* considerations. As time passes, memories fade, documents get lost, and a fair trial becomes increasingly difficult. There are also moral considerations. A statute of limitations belongs to that family of rights-of-the-accused on which a consensus has developed over the years. These rights include, for example, the privilege of interrogating one's accuser, the right to be represented by counsel, and the right not to incriminate oneself. The statute of limitations question in this case thus suggests two questions on the borderline between the moral and the legal. First, do the ordinary technical considerations apply when the crimes are so monstrous? And second, can statute of limitations protection be separated morally from these other traditional defenses of suspects who, even in the most dastardly of crimes, continue to be presumed innocent until they are proved guilty? Let us turn to each of these in order.

First, there is the relation, if any, between statutory limitations and the seriousness of the crime. Although there is some concept of a limit of time after a crime for prosecution, it varies widely from area to area and with reference to the type of crime committed. There have always been *some* crimes which in *some* places have no such limit. In the Commonwealth of Massachusetts, for example, and in many other areas, there is no statute of limitations on murder. Many countries, of which France is a notable example, have placed crimes against humanity, such as the ones for which the Nazi criminals are charged, in this category. This seems to indicate that the right in question is in no sense absolute.

(Incidentally, there seem to be no compelling *technical* reasons why the statute could not be extended in this case either. For a number of reasons, among them the Nazi obsession with keeping accurate records, there can be no question about the sufficiency of the documentation. Also, there is little chance that those who witnessed crimes of such monstrous proportions could sweep them from their memories even if they wanted to.)

But there is a second and seemingly more serious moral/technical question. Some German spokesmen have contended that, although the statute *could* be extended technically, it would be bad public policy. They argue that the Nazis themselves made a mockery of law by changing it to suit their whims and that the stability of the new Germany depends on a fastidious insistence that due process in its most stringent sense be observed. Under the Nazis, respect for the law fell to an all-time low. Consequently confidence in the law as an instrumentality beyond political pressure must be built up, they contend, if Germany is to mature into a real democracy.

The spirit of this argument, if it is an honest one and not an evasion, is commendable. The only hope that these crimes will not be repeated by future generations of Germans, or anyone else, depends not just on the punishment of past malefactors but on the development of attitudes and institutions which will prevent them. Certainly respect for the law is one of these attitudes. The difficulty with the argument, however, is that almost everyone agreed that a way to extend the statute without violating the constitution could be found. Eventually in fact it was found. The twenty-year limit was retained but the beginning date of the twenty years was fixed at December 31, 1949, the day the Allied Occupation Authorities gave West Germany authority to act as a sovereign power. Whether this solution affected German respect for the law adversely is of course impossible to say.

But a more general issue is the difficult one of how we can safeguard judicial procedures, especially those which protect people accused of horrible crimes, even when there is considerable pressure to relax them. Although many people were rightly repulsed by the statement by some German officials that in order to maintain the letter of the law we would have to "learn to live with murderers among us," in a more general sense this is true for any system which emphasizes the rights of the accused. Our American courts have decided time and again that if the protection of accused persons occasionally means the escape from justice of someone who is guilty, it is nevertheless justified on balance in order to protect innocent persons who might be wrongly punished.

Leaving aside the statute of limitations question for the moment, would not everyone agree that even those accused of crimes against humanity must be guaranteed all the rights of accused persons, including the persumption of innocence, difficult as this may seem? It is probable on a sheer basis of the large number of persons involved that there will be people accused of war crimes who are not in fact guilty of them. Would it be better to condemn them as the unfortunate price of getting all the culprits, or would we want to see their rights protected even if this might mean the escape from justice of some actual criminals? Does the fact that the crimes involved were so monstrous justify the punishment of even one innocent person? Probably most people would agree that the rights of accused persons apply regardless of the nature of the crime committed, and that if a small slippage of guilty persons is the price which must be paid for such protection, then it is a painful price, but one well worth paying. But the question is an ambiguous one and deserves careful reflection.

## Turning Guilt into Responsibility

Another question this debate raised, but did not answer satisfactorily lies on the borderline between theology and psychology. Given the fact of guilt, how can we avoid the two extremes of wallowing in it or escaping from it? How can guilt be faced and transformed into responsibility? In both the Jewish and the Christian tradition there is a strong emphasis on the fact that God *forgives* sin, that man does not have to bear the terrible burden of his guilt forever. This assurance of God's willingness to forgive and restore (*not* to "forgive and *forget*") excludes the two other alternatives. First, it excludes the possibility of a fascinated fixation on one's own guilt, an attitude which can make creative action entirely impossible. People paralyzed with guilt, or even luxuriating in it, are neither psychologically nor religiously whole. There is even considerable evidence that the perpetuation of guilt feelings in an individual or a nation can curdle the conscience and result in savage outbreaks of hatred and violence. Many historians believe that if the allies had bent every effort to help the German republic which came to birth after World War I rather than harping constantly on German "guilt," the psychological atmosphere which produced Nazism might not have developed.

But the other extreme excluded by the Judeo-Christian teaching on forgiveness is the glib washing one's hands of complicity, the refusal to accept the fact that one is guilty in fact and not just in feeling. Forgiveness allows no cheap escape from one's past.

Perhaps we need to ask this: what *does* the family of nations want Germany to *do* now about its guilty past? What can Germans do about this *now?* Certainly we do not want Germans to forget their past. That is why we should be sure that the Nazi period is adequately dealt with in textbooks, history courses, and literature. It is why Rabbi Joseph Asher's suggestion that a number of German-speaking Jewish rabbis spend a month each at German high schools teaching about Judaism is a good one. But neither do we want Germans to live in the past, fretting over it or fixated on it. Rather, we would hope that Germans would repent both individually and institutionally for their past offenses and accept responsibility for doing everything possible to prevent the recurrence of such things in the future.

If this is the case, then at some time, a word of forgiveness and restoration must be spoken to Germans, both individually and collectively. This word will have to be spoken, when it is spoken, by those who were most seriously hurt by the Nazis. In the April

20, 1965, issue of *Look Magazine*, Rabbi Joseph Asher of Temple Emmanuel, Greensboro, North Carolina, asks the question, "Isn't It Time We Forgave the Germans?" Rabbi Asher, who was reared in Wiesbaden and had to flee Hitler's Germany after a childhood scarred by insult and humiliation because he is a Jew, answers in the affirmative. He insists that bitterness must be converted into "the stuff of which civilized human relations are made." He goes on to say:

> Beyond retribution for evil lies compassion for the wrongdoer. "God desires not the death of the wicked, but that he return from his evil ways and live." That is the Jewish concept of God. Since man is created in His image, it behooves him to desire likewise. As wickedness springs from small and individual acts, thus does compassion begin in a single man's heart (p. 94).

It is interesting and significant that it is a religious Jew who was himself a victim of Nazism who says this. Only a person like him is in any position to decide *when* such a word should be spoken. Nor is the question of *how* such a word should be spoken something that can be decided either by outsiders or in advance, but it should certainly include an indication to the emerging generation of Germans that they will be received as full participants and responsible members of humanity and of the family of nations. (Germany is not yet a member of the U.N.) It would mean that the prejudice against all Germans that some Americans harbor, the one prejudice that we seem to allow ourselves after we have forbidden all others, must join color, religious, and other forms of prejudice on the ash-heap of attitudes unacceptable in morally sensitive persons.

This would not mean that we must approve of Germany's policies, that we must like all Germans we meet or that we must push all suspicions and painful memories out of our minds. It does mean that no one, whether he be a Negro, a Jew, a German, or an American, must bear the burden of living his life crippled and handicapped by the stereotypes projected on them by others.

It is never easy to forgive. Furthermore it is impossible for people who were not directly hurt by the Nazis to decide when and how those who were should make this forgiveness felt. But despite the enormity of the horrors perpetrated by Germans in the past, no serious adherent of any of the varieties of biblical faith could consistently claim that Germany should "never be forgiven."

Even more difficult is the plain biblical assertion that repentance often comes *after*, and not *before* forgiveness. God forgives Israel "even before they cried unto me." Jesus announces to men that their sins *have* been forgiven, they need only repent and live in the power of this forgiveness. In light of this difficult but irrefutable biblical insight, it must be said that those who have been hurt can elicit the repentance and wholeness they desire by making a move in the direction of reconciliation even before full and acceptable penitence has been accomplished.

But again let it be emphasized that Christians are in absolutely no position to advise Jews about forgiving Germans. Not only were Christians not hurt at all, in comparison to what Jews suffered, but worse than that, Christians have even fertilized the soil on which the poisonous flower of prejudice against Jews bore its monstrous fruit. The first responsibility Christians have therefore is not to call for forgiveness but to participate in the act of contrition.

### THE RELEVANCY OF THE GERMAN PROBLEM TO ISSUES CONFRONTING AMERICANS

Clearly the issues lurking just below the surface of the spirited discussion about the extension of the statute of limitations in Germany are deep and searching. Clearly they are issues which apply not only to Germans but to everyone. It is immediately evident, for example, that dimensions of this discussion find echoes in the contemporary American racial crisis. Every one of the questions we have listed as demanding further attention has its parallel in the complex relationships between Negro and white Americans.

The real issue in America, for example, is not how to punish those who have wronged Negroes in the past but how to create an atmosphere in which an interracial democracy can flourish. Part of the horror of our American tragedy is that Christianity has frequently been used as an ideology of suppression against Negroes. Some racists still talk about the "curse of Ham" and quote Scripture to undergird segregation. Many people continue to perpetuate unjust racial practices not because they have created them but because they have grown up with them and have not exercised the moral originality to question them. Thus the reality of corporate guilt by passive compliance complicates our racial picture in America as well as the German scene.

How often do we hear people claim that they personally bear Negroes no malice and do not see why white people today should be forced to pay for the sins and misdeeds of slave-owning ancestors. Yet we do all benefit from living in a nation built in part on slave labor, and this gives some substance, however small, to the claim of the Black Muslims that America owes the black man an enormous debt. Few people would agree that white America should turn over three states to the Negroes as the Muslims demand. Certainly the vast majority of Negro Americans would reject this idea completely. But there have been suggestions of a kind of Marshall Plan or GI Bill for Negroes, for compensatory training and a period of preferential hiring and these ideas are based on the legitimate notion that today's generation must pick up the tab for the bills incurred by a former generation.

Moral and legal arguments have also arisen out of the American civil rights struggle which bear a distinct resemblance to the statute of limitations discussion in Germany. Some people, in arguing against the public accommodations section of the Civil Rights Law of 1964 claimed, either seriously or speciously, that they opposed the bill because it involved a sacrifice of the owner's right to control property. Although this was hardly ever a serious issue in the minds of most people, since in both the American and the biblical traditions, human rights have a clear priority over property rights, nevertheless it did confuse some people for a while. More serious perhaps is the temptation we all have to forego legal niceties in hunting down and trying lynch mobs, racist murderers and KKK'ers. But in our best moments we all agree that even these people have the rights to counsel, due-process, and presumption of innocence which belong to every other accused person. We agree that the dastardliness of the crimes committed does not reduce the need to maintain these rights.

The question of guilt and reconcilation is painfully present in our situation as well as in Germany. How do white people avoid either wallowing in guilt or refusing to admit it? How do we avoid both the reverse racial jingoism which makes us laud all Negroes and suspend all criticism of them, and the endless machinations by which we avoid accepting the responsibility that white people share for the continued oppression of the black man in America today? Certainly with us also it must come from a stalwart facing and accepting of the guilt and then a deliberate movement *away* from dwelling on it and *toward* doing something to eradicate the evil it has produced.

Here too the Negro knows that sometime, somewhere, somehow an unambiguous word of forgiveness must be uttered. And white people know, or should know, how wrong it is for us to tell Negroes when or how this word should come. Perhaps the way it is coming in its more dramatic form in America today is through that remarkable movement of nonviolent direct action against racial injustice whose main symbol is the Reverend Dr. Martin Luther King. In some cases Negroes have shown a real willingness to proffer the hand of reconcilation. In other cases they have not. But in either case, the role of white Christians and Jews in this situation is clearly that of contrition rather than preachment, to be ready to accept the word of forgiveness when and if it comes, but to understand why in many cases it does not, or can not come.

134
30/-